THE
PUZZLES
OF
AMISH LIFE

Donald B. Kraybill

People's Place Book No. 10

Good Books®

Intercourse, PA 17534
800/762-7171
www.goodbks.com

Acknowledgements

Dozens of Amish persons kindly shared their time and ideas in my search to solve the puzzles of Amish life. I am deeply grateful for their generosity, helpfulness, and patience.

A Senior Research Fellowship from the National Endowment for the Humanities freed me from teaching duties to conduct interviews and complete the historical research. A grant from the Lancaster Mennonite Historical Society covered some of the expenses related to the interviews. Elizabethtown College (PA) contributed generous support in a variety of ways. The data sources and methods of research used for this study are described more fully in *The Riddle of Amish Culture* (Johns Hopkins University Press, 1989).

Barbara Strong Ellis, Becky Hagenston, and Stephen Storck offered valuable reactions to an early draft of the manuscript. In a splendid fashion, Jeanette S. Martin assisted with the editing and word processing.

Photo Credits

Cover: front—Blair Seitz; back—Richard Reinhold
Richard Reinhold—5, 7, 8, 9, 15, 16, 20, 26, 30, 33, 34, 40, 42, 47, 54, 61, 63, 66, 68, 69, 92, 94, 101, 102, 105, 112, 113, 114, 119, 120; Beth Oberholtzer—12, 14, 37, 80, 117; Gene Puskar—19, 74, 99, 110; Kenneth Pellman—22, 23, 44, 48, 49, 50, 51, 60, 72, 75, 76, 86, 96, 118; Blair Seitz—59, 67, 79, 82, 83, 88; Stephen Scott—89; Peter Bail—90.

Design by Dawn J. Ranck

THE PUZZLES OF AMISH LIFE
Copyright © 1990, 1995, 1998 by Good Books, Intercourse, PA 17534
First published in 1990
REVISED EDITION, 1998.
International Standard Book Number: 1-56148-001-0
Library of Congress Catalog Card Number: 90-71119

Library of Congress Cataloging-in-Publication Data
Kraybill, Donald B.
  The puzzles of Amish life / Donald B. Kraybill.
    p. cm.
  ISBN 1-56148-001-0 (pbk.)
    1. Amish—Pennsylvania—Lancaster County—Social life and customs. 2. Lancaster County (Pa.)—Social life and customs. I. Title.
F157.L2K73 1990
974.8'150088287—dc20   90-71119
                                                                                      CIP

Table of Contents

Introduction

Introduction

The puzzles of Amish life are many. Telephones, taboo in homes, stand at the end of farm lanes. Powerful tractors used at Amish barns rarely venture into fields. Horses pull modern hay balers and corn pickers on Amish farms. State of the art calculators are permissible, but not computers. Forbidden to own or operate motor vehicles, the Amish freely hire cars and vans for transportation. Electricity from public power lines is off limits, but 12-volt current from batteries is widely used. Clothing, styled in traditional patterns, is made from synthetic materials.

The unique blend of old and new in Amish life baffles us. Indeed, at first glance, the unusual mixtures look silly to modern folks. These perplexing puzzles, however, are quite reasonable when pieced together in the context of Amish history. Many of the puzzles are practical, cultural compromises—bargains that the Amish have struck between traditional ways and the powerful forces of modernization.

Amish settlements are scattered across 22 states and the Canadian province of Ontario. The following essays reflect the life of the Old Order Amish in Lancaster County, Pennsylvania, the oldest and most densely populated Amish settlement. The relentless press of urbanization on this community has produced a host of intriguing puzzles. While the details of Amish puzzles vary from settlement to settlement, the cultural values undergirding the puzzles in this book sustain the life of many other Amish communities as well. However, the specific examples are drawn from the Lancaster Amish.

1.
Growth

Puzzle: How do the Amish thrive in the midst of modern life?

Extinct in their European homeland, the Amish have flourished in North America in the 20th century. From a meager band of 5,000 at the beginning of the century, they exceed 150,000 adults and children today. The Lancaster settlement with less than 500 persons in 1900 has already passed the 19,000 mark. In many areas of life, the Amish cling to traditional ways—shunning electricity, cars and higher education. Yet they have survived, indeed flourished, in the face of modernization. Ironically, their growth paralleled the rise of industrialization. How did such traditional folks manage to thrive in the midst of modern life?

Three factors have contributed to their success: biological reproduction, cultural resistance and a willingness to strike compromises with the modern world. Groups that want to grow must replace their members through biological reproduction or outside recruitment. They must, in essence, either make babies or converts. The Amish do not actively evangelize or proselytize. They welcome outsiders into their ranks, but few have made the cultural leap. A high birth rate feeds Amish growth. Women typically give birth to seven children. Following the toll of death and disease, the number of children averages 6.6 per family. The rejection of birth control and the use of modern medicines have boosted Amish birth rates. Large families are typical in rural societies where chil-

The Amish have flourished in the midst of modern life.

dren are welcomed for their labor. Family size typically shrinks as families leave the farm. It remains to be seen if the Amish birth rate will slump as they leave their plows to work in small cottage industries.

Most Children Join

Large families, alone, do not assure growth. Children must be convinced to remain in the group. Widespread defections would, of course, offset any gain produced by high birth rates. The Amish have successfully kept most of their children. Estimates of the dropout rate in the Lancaster settlement vary from 10 to 15 percent. According to Amish leaders, more and more of their youth are embracing their religious heritage. In any event, four out of five children remain Amish. Why?

Amish parochial schools effectively socialize children through the eighth grade. The taboo on high school and college insulates Amish youth from modern values. Surrounded by dozens of uncles, aunts, and cousins, children are entangled in a warm web of family ties. Jobs, friendships, and business opportunities within the Amish community provide strong incentives to stay. The Amish have created an alternative society, an Amish world, that offers emotional security—meaning, identity, and belonging. These forces pull Amish youth toward membership and cancel out worldly tugs that might entice them away. Some, of course, do leave the ethnic fold, but the bulk of the children (85%) join the Amish church. The high birth rate and few defections have produced vigorous growth. Beyond natural reproduction, the Amish use a two-pronged strategy for surviving: cultural resistance and cultural compromise.

Resisting Modern Society

The Amish have resisted encroachment of modern society in several ways. They have translated many of their core values into visible symbols of identity—ethnic flags that mark off their cultural turf. Humility, modesty, obedience, equality, and simplicity are symbolized in plain dress. Such values are

Friendship, family, work, and play blend together in the Amish world.

also reflected in the horse, the buggy, and the lantern, as well as the traditional modes of farming. These stark symbols of tradition draw sharp contours between modern and Amish life. Their daily use reminds insider and outsider alike of the cultural fences dividing the two worlds. Moreover, these ethnic flags call members to surrender convenience, pleasure, vanity, and even personal identity for the sake of the group's larger mission.

The Amish also resist modern life by curbing interaction with outsiders. The use of Pennsylvania German as the child's native tongue shapes a unique world view, binds members together, and draws a sharp line between insiders

Amish ways often diverge from modern ones.

and outsiders. The dialect controls and limits interaction with non-Amish. The Amish do speak English, but the Pennsylvania German dialect or "Dutch," as it is called, reminds speakers that the ethnic community is their primary home. Horse transportation limits travel and hence, interaction with outsiders. Taboos on political and social involvement in community organizations also restrict social ties. The rejection of radio, television, and other mass media insulates the Amish from threatening secular values. Amish schools immerse youth in traditional lore and thought. The schools also remove Amish youth from the corrosive influence of worldly peers. All of these practices enable the Amish to resist assimilation into modern life.

A network of Amish institutions encircles members from cradle to grave. There are occasional trips to a non-Amish doctor, dentist, accountant, or optometrist, but, for the most part, members live in an Amish world. Work, play, worship, commerce, and friendship flow within an Amish orbit. The rise of Amish shops and stores provide jobs and shopping opportunities inside the Amish world. Buying and selling within the Amish network prevent money from draining off into the larger economy. The Amish, however, are not self-sufficient. They buy products, and especially raw materials, from outside vendors. The surge of Amish cottage industries has increased the scope of their community, making it easier for members to interact under the shadow of an ethnic umbrella. With these defensive practices, the Amish have fortified the cultural fences around their society and resisted the forces of modernization.

Compromising with Modern Society

The second prong of the Amish growth strategy is cultural compromise. The Amish are not a calcified relic of a bygone era. Part of their success lies in their willingness to compromise with modern life. Although resisting some modern ways, they have also willingly negotiated with the spirit of progress. The resulting compromises often baffle us, for they appear as odd mixtures of tradition and progress. The Amish don't own or drive cars, but they frequently ride in hired vehicles. Tractors are used around Amish barns, but not in fields. Community telephones appear at the end of farm lanes, but not in homes. Twelve-volt electricity from batteries is widely used, but 110-volt from public utility lines is forbidden. Horses pull modern farm machinery through Amish fields. Modern gas appliances, rather than electric ones, are found in Amish kitchens. Gas lamps illuminate modern bathrooms in Amish homes.

Sophisticated machinery pulled by mules reflects the delicate tension the Amish experience between modern and traditional life.

The list of cultural compromises is endless. Perplexing to outsiders, the bargains strike a delicate balance between the forces of tradition and the sway of progress. The Amish are willing to change, but not at the expense of communal values and ethnic identity. They are willing to use modern technology, but not when it disrupts family and community stability. The cultural compromises, rather than foolish contradictions, are negotiated deals that preserve key Amish values and, at the same time, permit selective modernization. They preserve the integrity of Amish identity while also tapping many of the benefits of modern life. They allow members to enjoy the best of both worlds. Such flexibility has enhanced the economic vitality of the Amish community and also helped them retain their youth. Biological reproduction, cultural resistance, and cultural compromise—the three major pieces in the Amish growth puzzle—have enabled them to flourish as a distinctive people in the 20th century.

2.
Separation

Puzzle: Why do the Amish separate themselves from the modern world?

The Amish are a friendly people. Yet they remain somewhat aloof from the rest of the world. Although their religious tenets emphasize separation from the world, they are entangled with it in many ways.

In the Amish mind, the "world" represents the values, practices, and behavior of the larger society. The term "world" symbolizes pride, greed, war, sin, and vice. An evil domain, the world threatens the purity and spiritual welfare of the Amish church. News reports of suicide, drug addiction, divorce, child abuse, terrorism, war, and fraud remind the Amish that they are indeed surrounded by an evil world. The term "world" conjures up negative images, examples of how not to live. What are the origins of this belief?

The Amish urge to separate from the world is rooted in their history. Their religious roots stretch back to the Anabaptist movement that emerged in Switzerland in 1525. The Anabaptists were a radical offshoot of the Protestant Reformation. Members of this new movement, seeking to be obedient to the New Testament, baptized each other as adults. They were nicknamed "Anabaptists," meaning twice baptized, since they had already been baptized as infants in the Roman Catholic church. Adult baptism, a criminal offense, was punishable by death. State authorities, as well as some Catholics and Protestants, joined in a campaign to eradicate the

Amish habits of dress provide a fence of separation between their community and the larger world.

Anabaptists. Thousands died for their religious beliefs in the years following 1525. They were tortured, starved, imprisoned, drowned, and burned at the stake. "Anabaptist hunters" were commissioned to track and kill members of this new movement that dared to challenge old religious and political ideas. The Anabaptists often held their religious services at night or in caves to avoid detection and death.

Seeking refuge from the bloody persecution, they moved into rural, mountainous areas for refuge. Many eventually became farmers. In 1693, Anabaptists in the Alsace region of modern-day France separated from the Swiss Anabaptists and began the Amish church. The division of 1693 erupted from a dispute over several religious issues: shunning excommunicated members, the practice of foot-washing, and the observance of communion. The Alsace group, led by Jacob Amman, eventually were called Amish. The Swiss Anabaptists gradually became known as Mennonites, a name derived from a Dutch Anabaptist leader, Menno Simons.

A Martyr Identity

The bitter persecution of the early Anabaptists left harsh memories. It galvanized the Anabaptist belief that the world despised the church. Many Amish today have a copy of the *Martyrs Mirror,* a thousand-page book subtitled, "The Bloody Theatre." Its text and drawings trace the bloody trail of martyrdom from apostolic times to the Anabaptist saga. As slavery and the holocaust shaped African-American and Jewish legacies, so the Anabaptist persecution engraved harsh memories into Amish history. A cautious stance toward the larger society has been handed down across the generations. References to the suffering of Christ, the apostles, and the Anabaptists abound in Amish stories, songs, and sermons. Biblical images of an evil world, as well as traditional Amish lore, underscore the wide gulf between church and world.

To maintain the purity, simplicity, and wholeness of their community, the Amish believe they must remain separate from the world.

Alternate modes of transportation separate the Amish from modern ways.

In But Not Of the World

The Amish maintain both symbolic and social separation from the world. Their dialect, unique dress, horse and buggy transportation, and lanterns separate them from the rest of us. Their hesitation to adopt the latest technological fads widens the gap between the two worlds. There are real social boundaries as well. Amish persons do not participate in public life—professional associations, community organizations, political parties, and public sports teams. Their business and legal partnerships rarely involve outsiders. Amish youth seldom attend public schools. Amish men, however, do join volunteer fire companies. They use parks and public recreation areas, but usually with a group of their own members. Although some vote in local elections, they do not hold political office. Their taboo on electricity protects them from secular values on television and other electronic media. A variety of ethnic institutions—schools, shops, and stores—insulates them from outside influences. Most of their life—work, worship, school, and play—revolves around family and church.

Despite their aloofness from modern culture, the Amish are entangled with the larger economic system. Although they shun government subsidies, they are not independent or self-sufficient. They lean heavily on the larger world for raw materials and supplies, as well as for markets for their products. They use banks and modern medicine along with many other professional services. Amish farmers buy fertilizers, insecticides, minerals, vitamins, and farm equipment from outside suppliers.

Although sidestepping electricity, they reach outside their community for energy—natural gas, kerosene, gasoline, and diesel fuel. Amish shops and cottage industries buy machinery and raw materials from suppliers in the larger world. And, of course, farmers, stores, and tourist shops sell their products and wares to the general public. Thus, as kerosene prices rise, Amish profits dip. And when milk and quilt prices

A contemporary lunch pail and traditional dress symbolize the Amish stance of being "in" but not "of" the world.

Amish values of simplicity and humility separate them from the pomp and circumstance of American life.

surge, Amish profits climb. As interest rates and land prices fluctuate, so do Amish fortunes. With the exception of social security, the Amish, like other Americans, pay their taxes. In all of these ways the Amish are tied to the American economy.

Like any group threatened by alien forces, the Amish have developed defensive tactics to protect themselves. Their unique dress, dialect, transportation, and farming methods mark the symbolic fences around their subculture and hold the modern world at bay. By controlling interaction with outsiders, limiting their participation in public life, and restricting the use of media, the Amish curb the impact of modern ways on their life. These defensive tactics help them preserve their unique culture in the face of modernization. By participating economically in the prevailing society, but not culturally, they have fortified their financial base while also protecting their community from the snares of modernity.

The Amish befriend outsiders and have congenial relations with non-Amish neighbors, but relationships with non-Amish rarely become intimate. Marriage to outsiders is forbidden.

Although they are personable and friendly, the Amish fear that a growing friendship with the modern world will, over time, erode their way of life. The Amish are good neighbors. They participate selectively in public community affairs—benefit auctions and disaster relief projects.

3.
Religion

Puzzle: Why do a religious people spurn religious symbols and church buildings?

The cultural roots of the Amish are religious. Many of their practices express a simple piety—a desire to be faithful to God. Religious meanings permeate their culture. Yet in many ways they do not act religious. They forgo church buildings, choirs, robes, altars, organs, and pews. Professional pastors, stained glass windows, steeples, offerings, and Sunday School classes are missing from Amish life. They do not evangelize, nor do they support missionaries. Yet they are religious. Why do such a religious people avoid many of the trappings of religion?

The Amish affirm the basic tenets of the Christian faith. Baptismal candidates are instructed in an Anabaptist Confession of Faith written in 1632, but the Amish put little emphasis on creeds. They believe that the Bible is God's Word and that Jesus was God's Son, who died for the salvation of their sins. The church, according to Amish beliefs, is the body of Christ fulfilling God's purposes on the earth. In addition to these convictions which the Amish share in common with many other Christians, they also emphasize the importance of keeping the body of Christ "pure and spotless" from contaminating stains of worldliness.

Amish faith focuses on daily practice rather than on creeds, sanctuaries, and abstract theology.

Faith Shapes One's Life

The Amish stress the importance of obedience, humility, and simplicity as fruits of a faithful Christian life. According to Anabaptist tradition, they believe that Christians are called to follow the nonresistant example of Christ. His followers should willingly endure suffering rather than retaliate. Christians, the Amish believe, should never use violence or resort to force. They should not file lawsuits or participate in the military, for doing so violates the meek and forgiving spirit of Jesus. When the demands of church and state collide, the Amish seek to follow the Word of God even when it results in humiliation or imprisonment. Finally, the Amish believe that religious faith should be practiced, not displayed. Following Anabaptist tenets, they seek to follow Christ in the practical affairs of life. They are a people who believe that

Fellowship and a community meal follow Sunday services.

faith should translate into daily living, rather than focus on creeds and sacred objects. Wearing plain clothing, living in a simple manner, and helping a neighbor in need are true expressions of faith for the Amish.

Some Amish practices date back to their Anabaptist beginnings. The radical Anabaptist reformers rejected the formal aspects of both Protestant and Catholic religion in the 16th century. The Anabaptists criticized priests of that day for corrupt teaching and loose living. Formal theological training, the Anabaptists argued, was unnecessary for true faith. Lay members of congregations should be able to read and interpret the Scriptures for themselves. The Anabaptists considered the use of images and sacred objects idolatrous, and they objected to the formal ritual of the Holy Mass. All of these practices, they believed, distracted from genuine worship. The heart of the individual and the gathered Christian community were the sacred ingredients of worship, not icons, crosses, and complicated rituals.

Church Services in Homes

Persecution by the established churches intensified the Anabaptist disdain for sacred rituals, objects, and places. The harassment forced the Anabaptists to go underground, making it difficult for them to hold services in public. Thus, the tradition of worshiping in homes evolved. Many of these sentiments and practices, ingrained in Anabaptist culture over the years, are still maintained by the Amish today. The Old Order Amish gather for worship every other Sunday for a three-hour service in one of their homes. Members of the congregation live in the immediate geographical area, or church district, bounded by roads and streams. Members must attend services in the district where they live. On the average, about 25 households or 75 adults, make up a church district. Including children, districts often exceed 150 persons. Worship services rotate from home to home in the course of a year.

Typically a bishop, two preachers, and a deacon lead each congregation without pay. The leaders are called from the

Amish Bibles, hymnals, and other devotional books are printed in the traditional language of the church, German.

ranks of the congregation and receive no theological training. Prior to baptism, young men promise to serve as a leader if called by the congregation. The bishop is responsible for the spiritual and administrative oversight of the congregation. He officiates at communions, weddings, funerals, and ordinations. The preachers are responsible to preach hour-long sermons without the aid of notes or special preparation. The preacher of the morning is selected by the leadership team a few minutes before he begins preaching.

The congregation sings, unaccompanied, from the *Ausbund*, a book of hymns written in the 16th century. Only the text is printed. The hymns are sung by memory in a very slow chant. One hymn may stretch over 15 minutes.

Women do not have public roles in the worship service, but they prepare and serve the common meal at noon. There are no special classes, testimonies, altar calls, printed liturgy, candles, or stained glass windows. The congregation sits on benches and chairs in several rooms of a home. They face the preacher who stands in a central area. The congregation kneels twice for prayer. The worship service is a common experience shared by young and old alike. It is a ritual reenactment of the values of humility, simplicity, and tradition.

Church Enhances Community

The simple practice of worshiping in homes, without the trappings of modern piety, shapes the core of Amish identity. It symbolizes the genuine integration of faith and life. Religion in the modern world is often relegated to special times and places—sanctuaries on Sunday mornings. It becomes specialized and separated from the other dimensions of life. In the Amish community, rotating worship services from home to home is a profound reminder that religious faith penetrates all aspects of living. Twenty-six times a year, members worship and visit in each other's homes and share a common meal. This routine weaves faith and life into a common fabric of meaning. In this context faith revolves around the corporate life of the congregation, not buildings, salaried staff, or programs. The plain and simple service in a home articulates important values from the Anabaptist past and distinguishes the Amish in the larger religious landscape. Worship in the home marks the Amish off from their Anabaptist cousins, the Mennonites, who hold services in church buildings.

Worship, family, and friends merge in an Amish funeral service.

Home worship has enabled the Amish to keep the congregation, their basic social unit, small. Because space in homes is limited, church districts must multiply as they grow. Thus, each person has a secure emotional "home" in a relatively small group of people. Members are known by first name. They become intimately involved in each others' lives in the overlapping circles of family, neighborhood, friendship, work, and play. These interwoven networks prevent persons from falling between the social cracks. One's absence at worship is noted. Family and friends are always nearby to celebrate birthdays and to assist in tragedies. Keeping worship at home has, over the years, assured that each member of the community has a secure niche in a dependable group.

Although the Amish disdain many of the outward symbols of modern religion, their faith permeates the entire fabric of their common life. It is a practical piety—one expressed by wearing plain clothing, raising a barn for a neighbor, and baking a pie for a friend. It is a religious faith anchored in the strength of tradition, rather than in emotional experience or ostentatious display.

4.
Humility

Puzzle: Why is humility a cherished value?

The rights and choices of Amish persons are restricted. Members cannot pursue higher education, enter professional careers, wear jewelry, or own televisions. Buying fashionable clothing, visiting a hair dresser, and purchasing a car are off limits. Yet the Amish appear contented and happy. How do they find joy and satisfaction in the midst of restrictive rules?

Obedience and humility are religious virtues in Amish life. Jesus' willingness to obey the will of God, even unto death, is the model for Amish obedience. Children are taught to obey their parents and teachers. Wives vow to obey their husbands at marriage. Faithful church members support church regulations. Younger ministers obey older ones. Disobedience, a cardinal sin in Amish life, is not tolerated. The sign of a rebellious spirit, disobedience mocks God's laws. If not confessed, it can lead to eternal damnation.

Individualism is Rejected

Pride also threatens community harmony. Proud individuals "show off" by elevating themselves above others. Many modern habits signal pride in Amish eyes. Jewelry, wristwatches, fashionable clothing, and personal photographs accentuate individuality and call attention to one's self. Modern folks work hard to call attention to themselves. By contrast, the Amish shy away from public recognition. They believe that attention-seeking leads to self-glory and eventually destroys community. Dress in modern life is used to

The power of community moves a stubborn, wooden beam.

express individuality and social status. It is a tool of individualism. By sharp contrast, ethnic dress in Amish life is a badge of group allegiance and identity. By wearing plain garb, Amish persons show their willingness to yield to group standards.

Humility is the hallmark of Amish ideals. Mild and modest personalities are esteemed. Patience, waiting, yielding to others, and a gentle chuckle are the marks of maturity. Modern culture, by contrast, stresses individual achievement, competition, assertiveness, self-fulfillment, individual rights, and personal choice. While other Americans work hard to "find themselves," the Amish work hard to "lose themselves" in the goals and activities of their community. Modern culture applauds independence, freedom, and egoism, while the Amish cheer conformity, modesty, and humility. Why?

Team work requires individuals to lay aside personal wishes for collective goals. From sports teams to armies, successful groups curb individualism. The Amish, to preserve their identity and to maintain harmony, encourage members to surrender personal aspirations for the sake of the common life. Pride and disobedience, to the Amish way of thinking, sow discord and endanger the community. Rooted in their religious heritage and reinforced by Biblical teaching, the values of obedience and humility funnel individual resources toward community goals.

The fear of individualism touches many dimensions of Amish life. Personal Bible study is discouraged because individual interpretations of Scripture might challenge traditional doctrine. Persons who show off their Biblical knowledge by quoting too much Scripture are called "Scripture Proud." Personal evangelism, personal devotions, and personal conversion are missing from the vocabulary of Amish religion, for they threaten to elevate the individual above the community. The Amish take a rather modest approach to personal salvation. In their minds, it would be arrogant to say that one is certain of eternal salvation. Rather, they yield to divine wisdom, call for faithful living, and believe that in due time God

Work at an early age teaches children to yield themselves to the larger goals of family and community.

will reward the faithful. The weighty matters of eternal life, they contend, are best left in the hands of God. It is their duty to live obediently and to trust in God's care. Personal testimonies, prepared sermons, and singing solos are viewed as egotistical expressions of vanity. God is pleased and honored, the Amish believe, when individuals quietly blend in with the common life.

Children are taught at a young age to "give up" their selfish will. The best way to "spoil" children is to let them have their own way. Living in large families with a half dozen siblings teaches children the importance of yielding to others. Cooperation rather than competition is stressed in Amish schools. Several lines of verse in an Amish school booklet capture their posture of humility.

> I must be a Christian child,
> Gentle, patient, meek and mild;
> Must be honest, simple, true
> In my words and actions too.
> I must cheerfully obey,

Giving up my will and way; . . .
Must remember, God can view
All I think, and all I do.
Glad that I can know I try,
Glad that children such as I,
In our feeble ways and small,
Can serve Him who loves us all.

The Problem of "Recognition"

Higher education, the Amish believe, leads to arrogance, pride, and a haughty spirit. The pursuit of humility continues in adult life. The Amish fear that publicity, luxuries, and large-scale business operations will make one proud. Some persons, for fear of pride, do not use their names when writing in Amish publications. Adults rarely grant interviews for public newspapers. The Amish shun publicity of all sorts since it fosters pride and calls undue attention to one's self. The Biblical admonition, "Pride cometh before a fall," is often quoted. Jewelry, makeup, and fashionable clothing are taboo since these tools of adornment highlight individuality. In a similar fashion, personal photographs are views as "graven images" which promote vain worship of the individual. Elaborate home decorating, professional landscaping, the latest gadgets, and gaudy, bold clothing, to Amish eyes, reveal a rebellious spirit trying to "show off and get ahead of others." Artwork that calls attention to the individual artist is frowned upon. Personal achievement is recognized quietly, with little fanfare and publicity.

Amish businesses do little, if any, advertising. Small and modest signs announce an Amish shop or store. Large farming and business operations are signs of greed. Church leaders fear that big operators will not only become proud, but will stir up jealousy and disturb the spirit of equality in the community. The gray color of Amish buggies is the color of humility, for it quietly blends into the surroundings. Regardless of income, occupation, or status, members travel to church in similar gray-topped buggies—a symbol of equality and separation from the world. Unlike mainstream culture, cars are not used to show off power, status, or wealth. In all of these ways Amish persons are called to give up their selves for the common welfare.

Community Preserves Personal Dignity

Talk of humility and obedience flies in the face of the modern obsession with individual achievement and self-fulfillment. Have the Amish created an oppressive culture that stifles human potential? The cultivation of humility is not a demeaning process in Amish life. They do not wallow in self-contempt nor champion wilted personalities. Individual dignity and personhood are respected. There are many areas for choice and self-expression, but the choices are limited.

The Amish believe that personal fulfillment is found not in assertive individualism, but in the context of a durable community. Losing one's self, for the Amish, is a redemptive process. For as they lose their selves in the larger mission of their community, they receive a firm ethnic identity and a secure emotional home in return. They have a people and a place. They know who they are, and that security compensates for the loss of some personal freedom. Their ethnic

Common standards of dress eliminate fad and fashion.

garb, distinctive customs, religious habits, and vigorous families confer a sharp sense of personal identity, grounded not in individual achievement, but in a religious and cultural peoplehood. The Amish believe that the joys of individualism are illusory. For them, the true roots of human fulfillment—meaning, identity, and belonging—are discovered in yielding one's self to the rhythms of the larger community.

5.
Shunning

Puzzle: Why do a gentle people shun disobedient members?

The Amish have been called "the gentle people." They are reluctant to use legal or political force in human relations. They applaud humility, charity, meekness, and patience. Yet they excommunicate and shun members who fail to comply with Amish practices. How can a gentle people be so stern?

Many churches practice excommunication, but the use of shunning, a social avoidance, is unique to the Amish. Jacob Ammann, founder of the Amish, was a Swiss Anabaptist leader. He believed the Bible taught that excommunicated church members should be socially avoided. This idea originated from an early Anabaptist Confession of Faith. The Swiss Anabaptists, however, did not practice shunning. Jacob Ammann became embroiled in a dispute with Swiss Anabaptist leaders over this practice. Other issues were involved as well, but shunning was the decisive one that led the followers of Jacob Ammann to separate from the Swiss Anabaptists in 1693. Over the years, shunning continued to be a distinguishing mark of Amish practice. Why should former members be treated so harshly?

Baptism Signals a Lifelong Commitment
The Amish stress the importance of adult baptism. In their late teens and early '20s, Amish youth decide if they want to join the church. If they choose to be baptized, they submit themselves to the order of the church for the rest of their

Excommunication removes deviants from the circle of fellowship.

The Ordnung specifies standards for Amish life and behavior.

lives. Candidates make a confession of Christian faith and agree to comply with the order and discipline of the community, known as the Ordnung. The unwritten Ordnung shapes Amish life and identity. Passed on by oral tradition, it spells out expected behaviors—wearing Amish clothing, using a horse and buggy, placing steel wheels on farm machinery, and using gas appliances. The regulations also forbid certain behaviors—divorce, going to college, attending theaters, filing law suits, owning cars, and using self-propelled farm equipment.

The baptismal vow is taken seriously; it is a lifelong religious commitment. Members who break it by transgressing the regulations of the church risk expulsion. Backsliders are given an opportunity to repent and confess their sins, but if they refuse, they are excommunicated and shunned. Amish youth who do not join the church are not shunned if they become members of some other church. However, a person baptized in the Amish church who later joins another denomination will be shunned. Baptized members who buy a car will be excommunicated and shunned if they refuse to sell the car and make a public confession. Offenders can always be reinstated into the fellowship upon repentance and confession, even in later years.

The rituals of Amish faith are designed to foster humility and repentance in the hope that excommunication can be averted. Kneeling is the posture of humility, for it shows respect for the authority of the community. Many religious rituals in the Amish life involve kneeling—public prayer, baptism, ordination, confession, and foot-washing in the communion service. In these sacred moments, the individual acknowledges the spiritual authority and supremacy of the community. Arrogant and rebellious individuals, who flout the teachings of the church and refuse to kneel, refuse to submit to the common order. They mock the spiritual authority of the church and risk expulsion.

Excommunication Done Reluctantly

The Amish do not expel persons quickly. They try to "win them back" and persuade them to cooperate with the church. A bishop emphasized the importance of love in the process. "If love is lost," he said, "God is lost, too. God is love. I sometimes think that love is worth more than fighting about this and that. You lose friendship through it." A young farmer is given six months to replace the rubber tires on his tractor with steel wheels. A businessman is allowed several months to complete a project before getting "rid of his computer." In some cases, wayward members are given a six-week, probationary excommunication while leaders seek to reinstate them.

Although the Amish hope to win wayward members back, they also believe that those who persist in disobedience must be banned from fellowship in order to maintain the purity of the church. To tolerate sin and worldliness would only breed more of the cancerous moral blight. Based on several Scriptures, Amish doctrine teaches that offensive members and open sinners must be excluded, rebuked, and purged from the church as an example and warning to others so that the church may be kept "pure from such spots and blemishes."

A Ritual of Exclusion

Shunning accompanies excommunication in the hope that backsliders will realize their mistake, repent, and mend their ways. It is a strong form of love designed to preserve the purity of the church, as well as to bring offenders to their knees in repentance. For the headstrong who fail to repent, shunning becomes a lifetime social quarantine. Members who refuse to shun other wayward members risk excommunication themselves. Those leading a wicked life are expelled from the church, shunned, and avoided by other members in eating, drinking, and other social matters so that the faithful do not become defiled by them and participate in their sin. Offenders are always welcome to return to the fellowship if they confess their errors.

Social interaction with expelled persons is restricted. Ostracized persons typically drift away from the church and community. If shunned persons attend a family gathering, they often eat at a special table to symbolize the exclusion. Relatives and family members must shun each other. Spouses may continue living together, but may not engage in sexual intercourse. Parents must avoid grown children who are

The Amish believe contentment lies in a well-ordered community.

The Ordnung *is transmitted orally across the generations.*

expelled. Members cannot be involved in business transactions with former members. If a shunned person must conduct business with a current member, a third party often handles the exchange of money. Members are not permitted to accept rides in the cars of ex-members. In both symbolic and literal ways the practice of shunning stigmatizes the disobedient, reminding members and deviants alike of the moral boundaries of the community.

The Amish believe that contentment and fulfillment are found in a well-ordered and regulated community. The rituals of excommunication purge moral blemishes from the community and rejuvenate the moral order. Shunning is a particularly effective form of social control. In the words of an ex-Amishman, "It works like an electric fence around a pasture with a pretty good fence charger on it." Although rarely used, shunning encourages those who consider breaking their baptismal vow to think twice. In Amish society, shunning means being cut off from all of one's friends and closest associates—a difficult process under any circumstance. It is especially painful in Amish society since virtually all of one's close friends and relatives are Amish. Shunning is, in essence, a cultural form of solitary confinement. "If it weren't for shunning," said one member, "many of our people would leave for a more progressive church where they could have electricity and cars."

Modern minds that cherish pluralism and tolerance balk at the thought of excommunication and shunning. However, businesses, schools, and public agencies readily dismiss employees who violate their policies. Communities are not afraid to imprison legal offenders. Even democratic governments imprison citizens who engage in treason. The regulatory mind-set is not unique to the Amish. They have merely applied it to the life of their community in order to preserve and purify its spiritual welfare. Purging the stains of worldliness protects the common life, encourages offenders to repent, and reinforces the moral boundaries of the disciplined community.

6.
Social Change

Puzzle: How do the Amish regulate social change?

The Amish are not a fossilized culture from a bygone era. On first glance they do look old-fashioned. Folks who spurn high school, shun cars, and read by lantern light are surely not modern. But in many ways the Amish are quite up-to-date. Farms use chemical fertilizers, hybrid seeds, and artificial insemination. Newer Amish homes are pleasantly furnished. They have lovely kitchen cabinets, modern bathrooms, and vinyl flooring. Amish shops and industries use elaborate manufacturing equipment. Many Amish retail stores have electronic cash registers.

The Amish have changed a great deal over the last century. Hydraulic water pumps have replaced hand pumps and windmills. Bath water, no longer heated in large copper kettles, is warmed by modern gas heaters. Wringer washers powered by gas or hydraulic motors have superseded hand-operated washers. Modern gas stoves and appliances stand where woodstoves and ice boxes once had a place. Spray starch, velcro, detergents, paper towels, and instant pudding are commonplace in Amish homes. Synthetic fabrics have made ironing nearly obsolete. In the barn, cows are milked with vacuum machines, not by hand. Large bulk tanks store and refrigerate milk. Old-fashioned, handheld plows have been completely mechanized. Amish farmers spray weeds and insects with chemicals from horse-drawn sprayers.

Each generation presses for new changes.

Openness to New Things

The Amish are not opposed to new things. They often snatch up new products along with their non-Amish neighbors. Amish mechanics have invented new products and creatively adapted old ones. The changes are endless. The Amish are not a static relic from another era; they are changing and evolving. What forces prod them to change? How do they control change?

The unwritten rules of the church, the Ordnung, control the speed of change. The Amish are slow to outlaw a new gadget or invention. If they think a new practice will harm the community, they will, in time, forbid it. They are, however, reluctant to reverse their minds a few years later. Decisions regarding the use of telephones and electricity made in the early decades of the 20th century still are binding today.

Many changes are prompted by economic forces. The use of indoor toilets was encouraged by milk inspectors. Bulk milk tanks and modern hay balers improved the plight of Amish dairy farmers. The use of air and hydraulic motors on large machinery in Amish industries enhanced their productivity. Other changes—modern kitchens and the use of synthetic clothing—were not spurred by economic factors. Many changes evolve because Amish persons, like the rest of us, aspire to a more comfortable and convenient life. Members who agitate for too much change, too fast, are called "fence jumpers." Deviants who openly violate traditional taboos or experiment too much are asked to confess their wrongdoing before the congregation. If they refuse, they risk excommunication.

Spotting Potential Trouble

New products in the larger society may meet several fates in the Amish community. A video camera and VCR are automatically taboo because they violate the long established norm against electricity and photography. Members normally are not tempted to use such products. Other items, however, are accepted without question because they fall in line with

The Ordnung *permits a plush seat but prohibits tractors in the field.*

historic practice and pose no threat. The chain saw and hand-held weed cutter, powered by two-cycle gas engines, were accepted with little ruckus since the gas engine had been a long-time fixture on Amish farms.

Other changes are ambiguous. Church leaders evaluate innovations, and those considered harmless slip into practice over time. Handheld calculators, running shoes, and barbecue grills gradually eased into use. In other cases, church leaders may deem the impact of a novel thing harmful and ask members to "put it away" and refrain from using it. This was the fate of personal computers in 1986. They required electricity, and leaders feared the computer might eventually lead to television. Practices or products which jeopardize the welfare of the community or challenge existing traditions are dubbed "worldly" in an attempt to keep them at a safe distance.

Taboo practices or products are not deemed immoral or evil in and of themselves. Church leaders consider the long-term consequences if a product is accepted. Might some detrimental ripples over the years disturb the life and welfare of the community? One bishop said, "There's nothing wrong with a car; the problem is what it will lead to in the next generation." Church leaders forbade the use of electric freezers in Amish homes because they feared freezers would lead to wider use of electricity and eventually to television. One member said, "It's not electricity that's so bad; it's all the other stuff that comes along with it." Accepting a computer, for instance, might make it difficult to uphold the taboo against television in the next generation. The Amish have an uncanny intuition for understanding how one seemingly innocent practice will lead to a more debilitating one later.

How Change Happens

The metaphor of drama, with backstage and front stage, clarifies the puzzle of social change. Front stage, public symbols are visible to both outsiders and insiders. Public badges of ethnicity, such as dress, symbolize the core of Amish identity and change very little. The colors and patterns of dress, the color and style of the buggy, and the use of horses are examples of public symbols. These are firmly entrenched in Amish life and highly resistant to change. Backstage, behind the curtain of public scrutiny, small changes occur rather freely. Clothing in traditional patterns and colors is made from modern synthetic materials. Thermopane windows and fiberglass are used to manufacture buggies with external shapes and colors that remain unchanged. Modern manufacturing equipment sits in Amish shops while horses plod across the fields. Hundreds of small changes happen quietly behind the curtain while the staunch public symbols, on front stage, protect Amish identity. Amish leaders across the settlement cooperate to preserve the public symbols. However, the pace of change backstage varies widely between church districts since it hinges on the policy of the local bishop.

Some changes occur deviously, as members keep the letter of the law but violate its spirit. In order to arrest the growing size of dairy herds in 1966, the bishops forbade using mechanical barn cleaners. In recent years, many farmers have liquefied cow manure to pump it by tractor into tank spreaders. They have not installed the mechanical cleaners forbidden by the bishops, but the liquid manure pumps enable

Newer Amish homes have a contemporary appearance. Small, adjacent barns often house a horse and a cottage industry.

them to handle an even greater volume more efficiently. In a gentleman's standoff, the bishops have politely looked the other way.

The Speed of Change

The pace of social change is restricted for a variety of reasons. Some limitations are designed to preserve labor and keep plenty of work for Amish children. Other lines are drawn to prevent the scale of things from expanding too fast and getting out of hand. Large farms and businesses would centralize power in the hands of a few people and threaten community equality. Some inventions are prohibited to arrest the speed of change. One member said, "We simply try to keep the wheel of change from turning too fast." Still other new products violate historic taboos of electricity, tractor, or car and have to be discarded promptly. Some changes are curtailed because they threaten to erode symbols of Amish identity. Other changes are bridled simply to protect the symbolic boundaries that separate the Amish from the larger world and other religious groups.

Ministers and bishops regulate the changes in all-day leaders' meetings held in the fall and spring of each year. Major decisions are taken back to local congregations for ratification. Leaders monitor rather than initiate change. In the late 1990s, some Amish youth began using roller blades. Church leaders did not object because roller blades were similar to roller skates—permitted for many years—and did not pose a threat to the community. A church leader did object, however, to youth wearing baseball uniforms and playing on local ball teams because this encouraged interaction with the outside world.

Change percolates from the fringes and margins of Amish society—not from the top down. Church leaders view themselves as "watchmen on the wall of Zion," on the lookout for little foxes of worldliness that might undermine the spiritual and social welfare of the community. They hope to shunt off debilitating change, but yet permit enough change to keep a healthy tension between the pull of tradition and the press of progress.

7.
Automobiles

Puzzle: Why is ownership of cars
objectionable, but not their use?

The use of cars is one of the perplexing puzzles of Amish
life. The Amish church has consistently objected to car ownership, yet the leaders permit their use. What reasons under-
lie this double standard? How can a religious people consci-
entiously forbid owning cars and at the same time allow their
use? The car puzzle emerged gradually in the 20th century.
Seen through Amish eyes, it is a reasonable way to cope with
the creeping pressures of modernity.

Henry Ford manufactured the Model T in 1908, and in the
next two decades the car became a common fixture in
American life. Indeed, it became the American symbol of
freedom and independence. The car provided *auto*matic *mobility* that revolutionized social life in the first half of this century. No longer constrained by walking, the slow pace of
horses, or trolley schedules, individuals could travel indepen-
dently whenever and wherever they chose. The car was the
child of modernity, for it embodied individualism, autonomy,
speed, freedom, mobility, and social status. In all of these
ways the car clashed with the traditional values of Amish culture.

A Challenge to Community Life

If the Amish permitted cars, their members would have
easy access to cities and other faraway places. Local church
districts, held together by horse travel, would begin to erode

Cars, vans, and trucks are often hired throughout the week; however, carriages carry members to Sunday services.

if members could drive away to the congregation of their choice. The speed of cars would accelerate the pace of Amish life. Members would have greater freedom to interact with outsiders and explore life in strange places. The automatic mobility provided by the car would surely promote individualism. Members would not only come and go as they pleased, but would use their cars as status symbols, threatening the social equality of Amish life. The car, in short, was a modern, worldly instrument that challenged core values of Amish life.

As cars gained in popularity, the Amish decided to ban their ownership. Some members declared that they would never ride in one of those "worldly contraptions," and they never did. Others rode occasionally with non-Amish neighbors. Over the years, however, the Amish attitude toward the use of cars relaxed. As one grandfather put it, "The use of cars is one thing the church has slipped up on." In the late '40s and the early '50s, the Lancaster settlement began expanding to several surrounding counties, making it difficult to visit family and friends by horse and buggy. Church leaders agreed to permit members to hire non-Amish drivers

Members of the community frequently use public transportation, with the exception of airplanes.

Numerous non-Amish earn supplemental income by providing "taxi" service for Amish business and social functions.

to take them to social functions—funerals, auctions, weddings, barn-raisings—on the outskirts of the settlement beyond the reach of horse and buggy. Gradual use of the car for these social activities was necessary in order to keep the larger settlement together.

Selective Use of Vehicles

The first "Amish taxi" service was inaugurated in the 1950s when a non-Amish neighbor began "hauling" Amish neighbors on a regular and paid basis. Today, dozens of non-Amish persons earn a living or supplemental income by transporting Amish persons to social and business activities. A dramatic rise in the use of cars and vans came in the 1970s as many Amish entered non-farm occupations. Mobile construction crews needed transportation to work sties, so they hired vans to take them on a daily basis. Amish craft shops and cottage industries began to lean heavily on hired vans and trucks to transport supplies and products.

Today, Amish businessmen often employ a non-Amish employee who provides a vehicle for business use. Vehicle owners are paid mileage for the use of their vehicles. In other cases Amish businessmen have standing agreements with non-Amish persons to haul materials as needed. Families will typically develop a relationship with several nearby "taxi" owners who "haul" them to stores and social functions when needed. Sometimes several couples may hire a driver for a week or more to visit friends or attend a business function—perhaps a horse sale—in a distant state. The expansion of Amish settlements and the rise of cottage industries accelerated Amish use of motor vehicles.

The Amish draw a sharp distinction between ownership and use of motor vehicles. Church regulations prohibit owning and driving vehicles as well as holding a driver's license. Amish businessmen are asked not to make loans to non-Amish employees for buying vehicles. Members are permitted to hire "taxis" (cars, vans, trucks) for a wide variety of business and social trips "when necessary." Hiring a driver for a pleasure trip is frowned upon, thus such trips are often combined with business. Church leaders strongly discourage the use of cars on Sunday, except to visit relatives in the hospital. This taboo maintains the horse as a symbol of Amish

Church members regularly hire vans and cars for business purposes. These vehicles are also used to visit family and friends beyond the reach of horses.

Trucks, owned and operated by non-Amish employees, are regularly used by Amish businesses.

identity since everyone travels to worship services by horse and buggy, or in some cases by walking. The use of horse on Sunday keeps an outward appearance of equality among members. It also keeps members of the church district tied to the local community.

The car agreement is a cultural compromise. Prohibiting the ownership of cars preserves the horse as a key symbol of Amish identity. As one amishwoman said, "Anyone that gets a car just isn't Amish." Another member observed, "The first thing people do when they leave the Amish church is get a car." The taboo on vehicle ownership supports Amish identity by marking a sharp boundary of separation from the larger world. The car taboo also keeps individualism in check. Members cannot come and go as they please; they must bend to the schedule of other drivers. Members do not experience the exhilaration and independence of a speeding driver freewheeling down the expressway. The compromise also prevents members from using the car as a status symbol to enhance their image in the community. By restricting use of the auto, the Amish have safeguarded the equality, stability, and identity of their community.

On the other hand, selective use of vehicles enlarges the social and financial base of the Amish community. Visits to far-flung relatives and trips to quiltings and barn-raisings fortify the community. The hiring of vehicles for a wide variety of business purposes strengthens the financial stability of the community. In all these ways the car puzzle, rather than being hypocritical, is an astute cultural compromise. It protects the traditional identity and equality of the community while allowing it to flourish financially and socially. It balances the need for selective modernization with the importance of tradition—a way of retaining the virtue of community as well as the convenience of modernity.

8.
Transportation

Puzzle: Why are some modes of transportation acceptable and others forbidden?

We have just noted the Amish distinction between owner-ship and use of motor vehicles. There are additional pieces to the transportation puzzle. Travel by rail is acceptable, but air travel is not. Scooters are permitted, but bicycles are off limits. Riding public buses is permissible, but not riding motor cycles. Snowmobiles and all-terrain vehicles are taboo. The mainstay of Amish transportation is, of course, the horse and buggy. How do the pieces fit together?

Amish communities are organized around church districts that encompass a small geographical area, often only a mile or so in diameter. The community is woven together by face to face interaction and frequent socialization. The circles of social networks overlap so that neighbors who work togeth-er also worship and play together. Horse and buggy trans-portation holds the local community together by restricting travel to distant places and increasing visiting in the immedi-ate locale. Modern forms of transportation speed individuals away from home. Indeed, cars are one of many factors that create "bedroom" suburbs where folks sleep, but flee to shop, work, play, and travel.

The puzzle of transportation emerged as Amish leaders tried to hold their community together, while at the same time they tapped some of the benefits of modern transporta-

Roller skates, roller blades, and scooters are faster than walking, yet do not allow traveling greater distances as bicycles do.

tion. Trains were widely used in the 19th century, and the Amish readily rode them. The train did not pose an immediate or direct threat to the members of the local community. As Amish migrations spread westward, trains were used by leaders to make fraternal visits between far-flung settlements. Although the train was a major advance in industrialization, it was not shunned by the Amish. It provided a public service and, unlike a car, a train could not be used for personal status.

The Amish also rode trolleys before cars gained widespread popularity. Like the train, the trolley was a public vehicle that could be used when necessary but did not threaten the well-being of the Amish community. Buses provided a valuable service for single women and widows who needed transportation for shopping and for working at market stands. Today both men and women use public busses for many purposes.

Lines Drawn Against Airplanes

Air travel, however, is a different story. In rare cases of emergencies, such as funerals, church leaders may give special permission for flights. Member who travel by air without permission may be asked to make a public confession before the church. When asked the reason for the taboo on air travel, church leaders explain that it's "just too worldly." Some modern practices are dubbed "worldly" in order to control the speed of social change and to maintain symbolic boundaries of separation from the larger world. The Amish have always used trains and continue to do so for long trips. If necessary, a group of them will hire a van. Air travel, as one bishop explained, "just isn't necessary."

Public buses, used for local travel, enhanced the economic life of Amish society. Air travel, by contrast, symbolized a modern mode of travel—one that was distant, abstract, and unrelated to the economic welfare of the community. Furthermore, it usually required traveling to a large airport near a major city. The acceptance of bus and train travel and the rejection of flying seemed a reasonable compromise in the Amish mind. Members could still use the bus and train, as needed. Because the Amish were not engaged in professional occupations that required air travel and since vacations to faraway islands and overseas resorts were not encouraged, air travel was simply unnecessary. The taboo on flying set a cultural limit, demonstrating that church leaders had not completely capitulated to modern life. It reminded members that there was a difference, a boundary, between the Amish and the larger world. Wise leaders saw the need for and allowed long distance travel, by train and van, but also reminded members that they were not free to just fly away at will. They were a separate people who could not completely embrace modern travel.

The Difference Between Bicycles and Scooters

Another piece of the transportation puzzle involves the bicycle taboo. Amish youth generally do not use bicycles. Tricycles and wagons are acceptable as are other small toys on wheels. Motorcycles, snowmobiles, and all-terrain vehicles are off limits since they symbolize pleasure and, like the car, would encourage individualism—automatic mobility, self-indulgence, and social status. One member of the church explained that the taboo on bicycles was established to encourage young people to stay around home. Young folks on bicycles could ride off whenever they pleased and avoid the watchful eye of parents. Old Order Mennonite groups, however, permit their youth to ride bicycles, and thus the Amish taboo also marks off the cultural lines between the two groups.

An interesting twist in the transportation puzzle in recent years has been the widespread use of scooters by young people, and even some adults. Many youth ride their scooters to school. The scooter represents a compromise between walking and riding a bicycle. Faster than walking but not as fast as a bicycle, scooters symbolize the delicate balance between the tug of tradition and the pull of progress. Scooters and other small equipment—wagons, tricycles, and wheelbarrows—may have rubber wheels.

Larger farm implements, such as tractors, wagons, and hay balers, roll on steel wheels. The Amish fear that the use of air-filled tires on larger equipment might lead to the car. Rubber tires, of course, run much more smoothly than steel wheels on macadam roads. Farm implements with rubber tires, the Amish fear, might be used to travel to town. The next generation might beg for pick-up trucks and the grandchildren for cars. The Amish have witnessed these evolutionary steps toward the car taking place in some progressive Amish communities that have eventually yielded to modernization.

The transportation riddle, puzzling outsiders, reflects the community's attempt to strike a delicate balance between tradition and progress. It is a balance that arrests the rapidly spinning wheel of change but also allows moderate use of modern travel.

9.
Tractors

Puzzle: Why are tractors permitted around barns but not in fields?

Tractors are common on Amish farms. They are used for power around the barn but not for field work. What sort of logic lies beneath this baffling distinction? By what divine mystery are tractors acceptable at the barn but not in the field? Solving this puzzle requires us to unravel strands of history.

By 1880 large steam engines were used to power threshing machines on many farms. Small gasoline engines were also used at the turn of the century to saw wood, pump water, grind feed, and power washing machines. With no objections to the internal combustion engine, the Amish, along with their neighbors, were using both steam and gasoline engines at the dawn of the 20th century. Horses were, of course, used on Amish and non-Amish farms alike to plow, cultivate, and harvest crops.

Although a few tractors appeared before Word War I, their use rose in the early '20s. The first tractors were heavy, awkward contraptions. Their steel wheels packed the soil, and they were difficult to maneuver in small fields. In many respects these early tractors were merely an extension of the steam engine. So perhaps it is not surprising that a dozen or so Amish farmers began using these clumsy tractors to plow and harrow their fields.

Tractors provide power to chop green corn and blow it to the tops of silos.

Second Thoughts About Tractors

Amish leaders, however, began to have second thoughts about the long-term implications of using tractors in the fields. After several years of debate, they recalled the tractors from the field and limited their use, as in the past, for high power needs around the barn—threshing wheat and blowing corn silage to the top of 30-foot storage silos. Several factors likely played a role in the decision to withdraw tractors from the fields in the early '20s.

First, horses held a clear advantage over the clumsy tractors. Horses were cheaper, easier to navigate in small fields, and they didn't pack the soil. Second, a few years earlier the bishops had rejected the ownership of cars. The tractors, although awkward contraptions, had some striking similarities. They were self-propelled and, like cars, could be driven about freely. Some bishops feared that the tractor might eventually lead to the car. If the church had rejected the car as too modern, how could it now turn around and bless the tractor? Third, Amish leaders had been rather tolerant in the first two decades of the 20th century. They had permitted

The use of steel wheels on tractors and other farm machinery discourages driving on public roadways and upholds the taboo on pneumatic tires.

Tractors have replaced steam engines for threshing wheat on Amish farms.

Amish farmers to purchase all sorts of new pieces of farm equipment—manure spreaders, tobacco planters, hay loaders—as they appeared on the market. In fact, Amish farmers were often the first in their neighborhood to buy the new equipment. Where might this all lead? Perhaps, the leaders reasoned, they should slow things down a bit and draw the line by keeping tractors at the barn. Finally, the shadow of an internal division among the Amish hovered over the tractor puzzle. A more progressive group, known as the Peachey Church, broke off from the main body of Old Order Amish in 1910. The progressive group began using some technological innovation: electricity, the telephone, the tractor, and eventually the car. It felt awkward, almost embarrassing, to the Old Order bishops to simply allow their members to follow the progressive footsteps of the Peachey group and take their tractors to the field. Thus, in about 1923, Amish farmers were asked to bring their tractors out of the fields and keep them at the barn.

After the Great Depression of the '30s, new all-purpose tractors appeared on North American farms. Smaller, with rubber wheels and greater versatility, they could be used for a variety of purposes. The lightweight tractors clearly held an edge over horses, and once again they tempted Amish farmers. By the early 1940s all-purpose tractors were being used on virtually all non-Amish farms. The temptation was too great; numerous Amish farmers took the tractors to their fields again. By this time the bishops were convinced that the newer, rubber-tired tractors were only a step away from the car. Citing the experience in other Amish communities, a member said, "Before you know it, they put rubber tires on the tractors and the next thing they are driving them to town for groceries. And the next generation grows up they can't understand the difference between using a tractor for business trips to town and a car, and so they get a car." Fearing this trend, Amish leaders recalled tractors from the fields again in the early '40s.

An "Amish Tractor"

But the lure of the tractor did not vanish. In the late '50s a new generation of farm machinery was coming on the market. The modern equipment was powered directly by tractor engines. The new machinery could boost the productivity of dairy farms. Amish farmers hoped to use the new equipment, but they needed a tractor for power. Ingenious Amish mechanics provided a solution. They developed a power unit, nicknamed "Amish tractor." The Amish craftsmen simply placed a large tractor engine on a four-wheeled cart and pulled the cart through the field with horses, for, as one farmer said with a twinkle in his eye, "We need the horses to steer it." The "Amish tractor" could be hooked up to various farm implements and power them as they inched across the fields. The power units were used for several years on some Amish farms, but the bishops were uneasy. They feared that in a short time the "Amish tractor" would lead to a real tractor, and the real tractors would surely lead to cars. So in 1966 the power units were banned from Amish fields.

The Horse Enhances Identity

In addition to the reasons cited above, several other factors have kept tractors at the barn. First, using horses in the field

An Amish farmer and his non-Amish neighbor work within view of each other in the fields.

helps to limit the size of Amish farms. Tractors lead to a never-ending cycle of expanding into bigger and bigger operations, which in turn must pay for more and more expensive tractors that today often exceed $40,000. Expensive tractors require more and more acreage to pay them off, and so on. Horses place a convenient limit on the number of acres a family can farm, thus promoting equality within the community and protecting the small family farm. Second, the use of tractors eliminates labor and speeds up the pace of farming. In contrast to most Americans, the Amish welcome labor as the heartbeat of the community. Tractors would steal jobs and push Amish lads toward non-farm work. Third, keeping horses in the field makes it easier to preserve the use of horses in the Amish community. If each family had only one horse for driving on the road, the horse culture might become endangered. Keeping horses in the field strengthens the horse culture and, in the long run, helps to keep the horse on the road as the prime symbol of Amish identity. Finally, the horse in the field also serves as the core symbol of Amish identity. It clearly sets Amish farmers off from their neighbors, marks cultural boundaries, and reminds insider and outsider alike of the essence of Amish life.

Today, modern tractors on steel wheels are used for a variety of power purposes on Amish farms. They blow silage to the top of large silos, power feed grinders and hydraulic systems, pump liquid manure, and spin ventilating fans, but they rarely venture into the fields. The Amish distinction between barn use and field use was, in essence, a way of freezing history. Powerful engines could continue to be used at the barn as they were at the turn of the century, but they would stay off the fields. In this way they protected the horse, which has evolved as the prime symbol of Amish identity in the 20th century.

10.
Farm Machinery

Puzzle: Why are horses used to pull modern farm machinery?

Like their neighbors, Amish farmers use modern hay balers. However, they use an old-fashioned grain binder to cut wheat for harvest. Non-Amish farmers, by contrast, drive large, self-propelled grain combines. Amish farmers cut green corn for silage with a corn binder adapted for horses while their modern counterparts use self-propelled forage harvesters. Both Amish and non-Amish farmers use similar equipment for harvesting tobacco since the process has seen little mechanization. The Amish, of course, pull their equipment, modern hay balers as well as old-fashioned binders, by horses. How did this intricate maze emerge?

In the first half of the 20th century Amish farmers and their neighbors used similar machines. As non-Amish farmers began using tractors, they still pulled traditional "horse-drawn" implements. As the tractor became commonplace on American farms in the '40s, manufacturers began producing heavier equipment designed to be pulled and powered by tractors.

Since 1950, non-Amish farmers have shifted to sophisticated implements powered by large tractors and self-propelled units. For a time, the Amish were able to continue in their traditional ways by buying "surplus" horse-drawn machinery from dealers and farmers around Lancaster County. Several pressures in the mid-'50s, however, brought new changes.

Mules pull a hay rake built for tractors.

An engine mounted on a state-of-the-art mower provides power to cut a thick stand of grass.

Amish farmers were gradually shifting from general farming to dairy farming. Farmers with eight cows doubled and tripled their herds. The modern baler, popularized in the '50s, solved both of these problems. By compressing dried hay into tight bales, a large volume could be easily handled and stored in less space. Amish farmers began purchasing new hay balers and pulling them by horses. Gasoline engines mounted on the baler at the factory provided power. An Amish farmer, reflecting on the introduction of the baler in the '50s, said, "I'm still surprised that it slipped into practice." Undoubtedly the baler "slipped" into practice because the monthly milk check was fast becoming the chief source of income for many Amish farmers. Use of the baler allowed them to compete with other farmers and expand their financial base. Horses continue to pull modern hay balers on Amish farms. By the mid-1990s some farmers were using state-of-the-art round balers hitched to horses.

Selective Use of Equipment

Corn is an important dairy feed. Green corn is cut, chopped, and blown into vertical silos where it ferments into silage. In the fall, dried ears of corn are husked, ground, and

A small gasoline engine powers a corn binder. The green corn is chopped at the barn and blown into a silo for storage.

mixed into dairy feed. Some of the Amish farmers who watched the baler slip quietly into use began to push ahead for larger, modern harvesters. They began pulling the harvesters with horses but powered them with the so-called "Amish tractor" described earlier. The bishops feared these new changes for several reasons. As noted before, they worried that the "Amish tractor" would eventually lead to the tractor and then to the car. Non-Amish farmers were already using the next generation of harvesting equipment—large, self-propelled combines and harvesters. Amish leaders believed that their members who were starting to use the newer harvesting equipment would eventually clamor for self-propelled units, and then for tractors and cars. Moreover, the modern harvesters would allow dairy farmers to expand far beyond modest Amish limits. In a series of special ministers' meetings between 1962 and 1966, leaders decided to ban the modern harvesting equipment from Amish fields with one exception. They quietly overlooked the hay baler. In some church districts members refused to "put away" the new equipment and formed a more progressive group—the "New Order Amish."

Amish Mechanics Create a Hybrid

Amish mechanics were tinkering with other changes about this time that forged a key compromise—one that increased the power of farm machinery while keeping the horse in the field. The compromise placated the concerns of the bishops but allowed farmers to increase their productive capacity. Amish mechanics began mounting engines on tractor-drawn implements. With an independent source of power, the implements designed for tractors would now be pulled by horses. In 1960, gasoline engines were mounted on corn binders to cut green corn for silage. This increased the binder's speed and capacity. By installing gasoline engines and making other adaptions, the Amish were able to pull the tractor-designed implements with horses. Engines were installed on the hay crimper in 1960, the corn picker in 1965, the hay mowers in 1966, and in later years on the rotor beater and other equipment.

In a second development, Amish shops began manufacturing some of their own machinery. Today, they produce manure spreaders, wagons, corn planters, plows, sprayers, and many other horse-drawn implements. The grain binders

Modern hay balers pulled by mules symbolize the delicate balance between modern and traditional ways.

have seen little change. Old-fashioned binders, without engines, are still used to cut wheat. The declining importance of wheat in the local farm economy weakened pressure to change the binder. Today the Amish use two types of farm equipment: (1) modern machinery produced by commercial manufacturers and adapted for horse use, and (2) implements designed and manufactured in Amish shops. In rare instances, such as the grain binder, old-fashioned, horse-drawn equipment is still used.

Keeping the Symbolic Horse

Pulling modern implements with horses forged a unique compromise between progress and tradition. This unusual marriage keeps the horse—a symbol of Amish identity—firmly entrenched on Amish farms. In fact, one of the senior bishops, when asked about new equipment, was fond of saying, "You can have it, if you can pull it with horses." His adage underscored the symbolic importance of the horse as well as its practical significance. By keeping the horse in the field, Amish leaders were able to limit the size of Amish farms and thwart expansion. Although Amish farmers enhanced their productivity, they were not able to match the volume of their non-Amish neighbors who were using large, self-propelled equipment. Mounting engines on machinery increased productivity, but it also preserved manual labor and protected jobs which otherwise might have been snatched away by a full embrace of modern equipment. Automatic bale loaders, for instance, are not permitted on hay balers.

The acceptance of bulk milk tanks, but the rejection of silo unloaders, barn cleaners, and pipeline milking equipment is still another compromise which permits expansion within clearly specified limits. By manufacturing farm machinery, the Amish have created a whole new industry that provides hundreds of jobs for fellow church members. Pulling modern machinery with horses strikes a delicate balance. It is a compromise that sustains Amish tradition and identity while allowing just enough progress for farmers to remain competitive.

11.
Telephones

Puzzle: Why are telephones banned from
Amish homes?

The telephone is a taken-for-granted necessity in modern
life. The Amish ban phones from their homes, but they do
use public telephones and often have a "phone shanty" at the
end of a farm lane or at the side of a shop. What could be dan-
gerous about such an innocent bit of technology? How do the
pieces of the phone puzzle fit together? The solution to this
puzzle, as with many of the other puzzles of Amish life, lies
in a web of historical events.

Early Phones Removed
The telephone, invented in 1878, gradually came into use
in the first quarter of the 20th century. But even as late as
1940, only half of the farmers in Pennsylvania had one. In the
first decade of the century, the Amish tinkered with phones
along with some of their rural neighbors. Some Amish farmers strung homemade telephone lines between two or three
farmhouses and talked with each other on a primitive phone
system. An old church member recalls those days: "I remember when the phones came. The church didn't say anything
about them. It was thumbs up. Two of my wife's uncles had
the phones in, and there were quite a few others that had
them in. Then an issue came up. Two people talking on the
phone were gossiping about someone else, and it went so far
as to become a church issue. They were asked to come to
church and make a confession about it. And then the church

The placement of telephones in Amish businesses varies by church district. Some districts permit phones in offices, others, adjacent but outside, and still others, apart from buildings.

decided that we just better not allow these phones." Another Amish leader said that "around 1908 the bishops decided that the phone should be put away, and those involved in it just dropped it and tore the lines out." Amish leaders today are not exactly sure why the phone was banned from homes in those early days. Its use was never forbidden, but installing a phone was viewed as too worldly, a modern convenience that promoted gossip.

Several factors likely clinched the phone taboo. A division among the Amish in 1910 resulted from a disagreement over shunning. The progressive Peachey church that broke off from the Old Order Amish soon began installing phones in their homes. This tightened the Amish ban on the phone since Amish leaders wanted to keep a respectable social distance from the "liberal" group. The phone became a symbol of progressive worldliness which Amish elders hoped to avoid. When asked about the reason for rejecting the phone, a leader recently said, "It's something that's left over from the 1910 division." The phone, in essence, became one of several symbols that marked the social boundaries between the Old Order Amish and their progressive offshoots.

There were other reasons for placing a taboo on the phone. Rural America in 1910 lacked good roads. It had few automobiles, little electrical service, no radios, and poor postal service. On farms isolated from the rest of the nation, the telephone became a literal and symbolic link to the outside world. It would have tied the Amish to the larger society, thus violating their principle of separation from the world.

Phones Threaten Visiting

Furthermore, the telephone threatened to undermine the fabric of Amish life. Social relations were woven together by face-to-face conversations. Telephone talk would remove conversation from the rich symbolism of face-to-face interaction. Body language, facial expression, and dress codes—all so important in Amish culture—would be stripped away in phone conversations. Phone messages were, in essence, half-messages, emptied of nonverbal codes of meaning. Mechanical and impersonal, the phone was fitting for rational, secondary relationships, but not for intimate ones. Moreover, the phone threatened to erode visitation in Amish life. If one could call, why take the time to visit? In all of these ways the phone endangered the role of face-to-face chatter, the social adhesive of Amish life.

The phone interrupted the natural rhythm and spontaneous flow of family life. It provided automatic access to the larger world and allowed outside visitors to freely intrude into Amish homes. Interaction with outsiders normally occurred in a public setting under a watchful eye of other Amish neighbors. A telephone in each home would allow members to converse with outsiders without community surveillance. The phone was an unwanted link to the outside world. For all these reasons the Amish have for bidden the installation of phones in their homes. Using phones in public places or in homes of non-Amish neighbors, however, has always been permitted.

Community Phones Come Into Use

In the last half of the 20th century, a number of factors changed the pattern of phone use outside Amish homes.

Public telephones are used by members of the community.

A private phone booth serves an Amish business.

Farmers felt increasingly awkward walking into non-Amish kitchens as their neighbors became affluent. As the community purchased more farms, it became difficult to "borrow" a neighbor's phone since Amish families were often surrounded by other Amish farms. In the '50s, dairy herds expanded, and farmers needed to call veterinarians and feed dealers. Doctors and dentists increasingly required Amish patients to make appointments by telephone. The development of new Amish settlements in other counties and states encouraged phone use for emergencies such as funerals and accidents. All of these factors gave rise to the so called "community" phone. A "phone shanty," similar in appearance to an outhouse, was often built at the end of a farm lane. Several Amish neighbors shared the common phone to make outgoing calls.

Phone numbers for these community telephones are typically not listed in a public directory. Families share the expense of the phone. Since 1960 the number of community phones has surged. The phone shanties permit selective and controlled use of modern technologies. With the phone a considerable distance from the house, it can be used as needed to place outgoing calls, but rarely for incoming ones.

Another compromise of sorts, it permits careful use without allowing the ring of the phone to disrupt family life. The community phones are a communal solution that stands in stark contrast to the individualistic American dream of a portable phone in every car and on every belt.

Phones and Amish Businesses

The rise of Amish shops and cottage industries in the '70s and '80s added new demands for phones. Businessmen needed them to order supplies and receive orders for their products. Phones were often placed in small buildings outside shops.

The pattern of telephone use today varies by church district. Some local bishops tolerate phones in shops; others do not. Occasionally Amish shops will have multiple extension phones inside their offices, but in other districts they are strictly forbidden. Some farmers have installed phones in their barns, tobacco cellars, and garages. Despite these gradual changes, the church has held a firm line against phones in homes. With ample public phones, as well as numerous community phones, members routinely use the phone to make appointments, call Amish taxi drivers, contact veterinarians,

A private telephone booth stands near an Amish home.

and conduct business. The phone is increasingly being used within the Amish community. Members sometimes have certain hours when they are "nearby" their barn or shop phone to receive calls from each other. In other cases, members make "appointments" to call each other. Answering machines have also increased telephone use.

The Amish have asserted their control over the phone by keeping it at a distance. They use it as needed but are unwilling to let it disrupt their lives. They are its master, not its servant. The development of "community phones" has been an interesting compromise with modernity. The Amish have agreed to use the phone on their own terms, in ways that bolster their economic well-being and in collective ways that enhance the community. It is not permitted to foster individualism or indiscreet interaction with the outside world. Banning the phone from the home remains an important symbol of separation from the world, as well as a continuing marker that sets the Amish off from more "liberal" church groups.

12.
Electricity

Puzzle: Why are some forms of electricity acceptable while others are rejected?

The electricity puzzle is a complicated one. Electrical appliances and lights are missing from Amish homesteads and shops. Gas-pressured lanterns, similar to Coleman camping lamps, illuminate Amish homes and barns. Electrical equipment is rarely used in Amish shops, yet the Amish do use electricity. Batteries power lights, signals, and blinkers on Amish buggies. Some elderly members use battery operated lights for nighttime reading. Electric fences encircle Amish pastures, and electric motors stir the milk in Amish bulk tanks. Flashlights are widely used. Electric welders are commonplace in Amish machine shops. Many retail stores have electric cash registers.

Power Lines Pose a Problem

A variety of factors have shaped this perplexing puzzle. The Amish readily accepted batteries as they came into use at the turn of the 20th century. Being self-contained, the batteries were unconnected to the outside world. Electrical power companies were a different story. In the first two decades of the century, electrical usage was concentrated in cities. Several developments spurred its use into outlying rural areas and influenced the Amish response. First, some non-Amish farmers and small businesses set up their own electrical generating plants. Powered by gasoline engine, the generating plants provided electricity for light bulbs and

Amish retail stores often use electronic cash registers operated by electric inverters.

other electrical uses. As with the phone, the progressive Peachey Church, which separated from the Amish in 1910, began using generating plants. Amish leaders were reluctant to accept a new invention which the liberal group embraced warmly. Second, public utility lines began taking electricity into rural areas along major roads. Like the telephone line, electrical lines provided a literal and mysterious connection to the outside society. This tie clashed with the Amish principle of separation from the world. Accepting electricity from public utility lines would have linked the Amish directly to a larger society that they viewed with caution and suspicion.

The early decades of the century bustled with technological change as the car, telephone, radio, airplane, tractor, and electricity entered modern life. The Amish were wary of being swept along by the swift currents of progress. They were unsure of where all these changes might lead. Moreover, a senior bishop in the Amish church felt strongly that the use of electricity would lead the church astray. His influence undoubtedly played a major role in shaping the decision. For all of these reasons, the Amish taboo on electricity crystal-

By rejecting 110-volt electricity, the Amish have turned their backs on television.

lized around 1920. The use of electric lights, generating plants, and electricity from public utility lines were all forbidden. Leaders agreed, however, to continue the use of batteries as they had in the past.

As electrical usage in the wider society became standardized in the 20th century, direct current (DC) stored in batteries was typically the 12-volt variety. Alternating current (AC), available from public utility lines, was normally 110-volt. Thus over the years, the Amish accepted the use of 12-volt current stored in batteries but rejected the use of 110-volt alternating current. This distinction hardened as church leaders saw the avalanche of modern, 110-volt conveniences—radios, television, and appliances—spreading across society. Indeed, for a people who wanted to remain separate from the world, the taboo on 110-volt electricity began to make a lot of sense. The rejection of 110-volt current maintains a symbolic distance from the larger society, but it also cuts off the influence of outside media like radio and television, as well as the whole array of modern gadgets which would undermine the simplicity of Amish life.

What About Bulk Milk Tanks?

Although the Amish have maintained the taboo on 110-volt current, they have made several compromises over the years. In the late '60s, Amish dairy farmers were asked by milk companies to install large bulk tanks to store and refrigerate their milk. In the past, Amish farmers had stored and shipped their milk in cans. The milk companies insisted on the installation of bulk tanks and threatened to terminate farmers who refused. The Amish were in a quandary because the bulk tanks required electricity. In a series of meetings, Amish leaders and representatives of the milk companies hammered out a compromise. The Amish agreed to install bulk milk tanks if they could use diesel engines to operate the refrigeration units. They also agreed to install automatic agitators to stir the milk if they could use 12-volt motors powered by 12-volt batteries. The batteries were periodically recharged by a generator attached to the diesel engine. In the end, both parties were satisfied and a deal was struck.

New Electrical Lines

Electric welders became a necessity in the '70s as Amish shops were adapting modern farm machinery for horse use on a wide scale basis. Other shops were beginning to manufacture farm equipment. Moreover, farmers themselves needed welders to repair machinery on their farms. But welders required a source of electricity. Under growing pressure, church leaders agreed to permit electric generators operated by gasoline engines to power welders. Amish leaders feared, however, that farmers might begin plugging other electrical motors and equipment into their generators. Thus generators were restricted to powering welders and charging batteries. Mobile carpentry crews may use generators on construction sites to run electric power tools. The carpenters also use standard electric power tools if electricity is available on the site.

In the 1980s another electrical compromise of sorts developed. Some shop owners and farmers discovered that they could transform 12-volt current into "homemade" 110-volt

Amish-made batteries are used to start diesel engines on farms and in cottage industries.

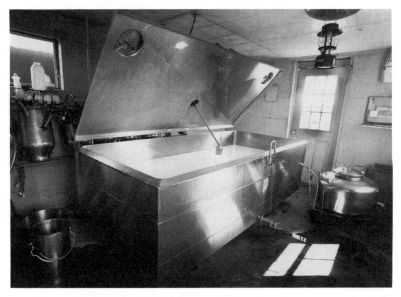

A lantern provides light in a milkhouse while a 12-volt motor stirs the milk. Vacuum milking machines are widely used.

electricity with an electrical device called an inverter. Roughly the size of a car battery, the inverter converts 12-volt electricity from batteries into 110-volt current to operate cash registers, typewriters, and other small appliances. The inverters, on one hand, respect Amish tradition since their source of electricity is indeed a 12-volt battery. However, on the other hand, the 110-volt current they produce can be used to power retail scales and small gadgets like soldering guns. The inverters provide a route around the traditional Amish taboo on 110-volt electricity. But they have serious limitations because they rarely have more than one or two outlets and can only power small appliances. Nevertheless, they are used in a variety of creative ways to operate electrical appliances ranging from cash registers to cow clippers. The inverters are a unique adaption that preserves Amish tradition, yet provides room for change within certain limits. As one person put it, "The inverters are still on probation." Their use varies widely across church districts, depending on the tolerance of the local bishop.

Current Practice

Batteries and 12-volt motors are widely used today for a variety of applications in homes, shops, and barns. With the exception of the welder and inverter, 110-volt current is frowned upon and rarely used. Pressurized gas lanterns are mounted on walls, hung from ceilings, and attached to mobile carts. They provide adequate lighting in Amish shops and homes. Indeed, the lantern has become one of the public symbols of ethnic identity in Amish life. The electrical taboo maintains a symbolic separation from the world and prevents the secular values carried by television and radio from intruding into Amish homes. Moreover, the taboo on electricity has been a shrewd way of arresting social change. It has silenced endless debate over the use of new electrical gadgets that have flowed into modern life in recent decades. In all of these ways, the electrical taboo has helped to preserve Amish culture.

13.
Power

Puzzle: How is modern machinery operated without electricity?

The Amish taboo on standard 110-volt electricity promoted a search for other forms of power. As noted earlier, the Amish used small gasoline engines for a variety of tasks from pumping water to running washing machines at the turn of the century. More recently, chain saws, weed trimmers, and other handheld tools powered by gasoline engines are widely used. In the '50s farmers began using industrial type diesel engines for power on their farms and shops. The diesels were used to operate refrigeration units on milk coolers as well as vacuum pumps for milking machines. With the arrival of large, bulk milk tanks in the late '60s, diesel power plants became commonplace on Amish farms.

Amish Inventors Preserve Tradition

The dramatic rise of machine shops and other cottage industries in the late '60s and '70s created a new problem. How could shop owners use drill presses, saws, sanders, grinders, and other machinery without electricity? Ingenious Amish mechanics found a creative solution which respected the historic taboo on electricity and also provided power for sophisticated tools and machinery. The mechanics discovered they could remove electric motors from commercial shop tools and replace them with air or hydraulic motors. The electric motor on a modern table saw or drill press was simply exchanged for an air or hydraulic motor. Air motors were

Windmills, used to pump water over the years, are being replaced with pneumatic water pumps.

powered by air pressure piped to the motor from an air pump attached to the diesel power plant. Oil under high pressure was forced to a hydraulic motor by a hydraulic pump operated by a diesel. In other words,the diesel engine operated pumps which sent either air or oil to the motors that powered the shop tools.

Today, Amish manufacturing enterprises, carpentry shops, and a variety of cottage industries use sophisticated equipment powered by air or hydraulic motors. Some of the larger machines operate directly from the power shaft of the diesel engine. This happy solution of "Amish electricity" pays polite courtesy to the traditional taboo on electricity while empowering Amish shops with a high level of productivity. Some shop owners are convinced that both hydraulic power and air power are cheaper and more efficient than electricity.

Farmers have also begun using hydraulic and air motors to power small equipment around the barn—ventilating fans, cow clippers, and hay elevators. Hydraulic pumps are replacing windmills and water wheels to pump water on many farms. Air and hydraulic are occasionally used to operate household equipment. Some washing machines are powered by small gas engines while others use air or hydraulic motors. A bake shop uses a hydraulic motor to operate a cake mixer. A young farmer hoped to "rig up" a hydraulic cake mixer for his wife. In some cases, sewing machines are powered with air motors.

"Amish Electricity"

Today, the typical Amish homestead has a diesel power plant operating a variety of motors and equipment. Generators to recharge batteries, as well as air and hydraulic pumps, are operated by the diesel. The air and hydraulic pumps feed a network of hoses that supply air and oil pressure to motors scattered around the homestead. A young shop owner summed up the changes, "We can do anything with air and hydraulic that you can do with electricity— except operate electronic equipment." Clearly the unwritten

Apart from electrical wires, outlets, and switches, newer Amish homes have a contemporary appearance.

understanding in Amish culture reads, "If you can do it with air or oil, you may do it!" The use of oil and air power is often jokingly called "Amish electricity" by the Amish themselves.

Although air and hydraulic pressure can be used to operate larger household equipment such as washer and sewing machines, it is not fitting for smaller electrical appliances. Without electricity, Amish homes lack clothes dryers, toasters, blow dryers, microwaves, televisions, VCRs, and doorbells. Newer ranch-style homes look remarkably modern on the outside. Inside they contain modern kitchens with beautiful carpentry, vinyl flooring, and formica counters. Bottled gas is used to operate major appliances such as refrigerators, stoves, and water heaters. Newer Amish homes have the latest models of gas ranges and stoves in a variety of colors. Their use of air or hydraulic power, however, remains concentrated in the barn and shop where it helps "to earn a living," rather than in the home where hand labor is more acceptable.

What About Home Freezers?

The use of home freezers is one of the more interesting pieces of the power puzzle. Large Amish families have always depended on large gardens. Canning is their primary way of preserving food. The availability of home freezers in The '50s provided a dilemma for the Amish. It was a technological innovation which certainly supported Amish values—large families, abundant food, and self-sufficiency. Freezers aided and eased food preparation for large families. Yet the use of freezers would violate the historic taboo on electricity.

Nevertheless, in the early '60s, some adventuresome farmers bought freezers and hooked them up to their electric generators powered by diesels. Although sympathetic to the merits of freezers, church leaders worried that they would quickly lead to other electrical appliances. What would keep farmers from plugging toasters, shavers, and even televisions into their generators? To block this worrisome trend, church leaders forbade home freezers in 1966, the same time that modern forage harvesters and combines were banned.

Although most families still preserve large quantities of fruits and vegetables by canning, some do use freezers. In recent years a few families have purchased gas freezers, but these are quite expensive. Many families rent freezer space at public produce markets and stores. Other families have an electric deep freezer space placed in the garage or basement of a non-Amish neighbor. The Amish family barters produce or some other service in exchange for space and electricity. Church leaders have permitted this interesting compromise since it allows families to store frozen produce nearby but at the same time keeps electrical outlets out of Amish homes. Like the telephone, this compromise is a way of selectively using modern technology while keeping it at a respectful dis-

A variety of hand tools are operated by air pressure in cottage industries.

Old-style wringer washing machines are powered by modern gasoline engines.

tance so it cannot undermine Amish values or lead to more troublesome gadgets.

The Amish power puzzle includes a variety of cultural compromises which permit the Amish to selectively adopt some modern technology. Community control of its use assures that the technology will not endanger the core of Amish life. The electrical taboo preserves a symbolic and literal boundary of separation from the larger world. It protects the lantern as a symbol of Amish identity and guards Amish homes from the intrusion of mass media. Moreover, the absence of electricity generates ample work for Amish children. Thus the power compromise preserves Amish values and identity while also providing a comfortable lifestyle and a secure economic base.

14.
Occupations

Puzzle: Why are some occupations acceptable and others taboo?

Farming has been the core of Amish life for nearly three centuries. In recent years, the Amish have entered a host of new occupations—cabinetry, mechanics, manufacturing, retailing, and crafts. However, hundreds of occupations are still off limits. How are occupations sorted into acceptable and unacceptable categories? Will the shift to new occupations change Amish life?

The Swiss Anabaptists, the religious ancestors of the Amish, moved into remote rural areas to avoid harsh persecution. Over the decades, the character of Amish life revolved around agriculture. Rural living reinforced and nurtured their religious outlook and piety. In Amish eyes, the newborn calf, the freshly plowed soil, the ripening grain, and even the hailstorm were manifestations of God's power. In their daily encounters with nature they communed with God. Farming was not merely a job or career, it was a way of life anchored in the Scriptures, blessed by God, and handed down over the generations by Amish ancestors. The very fabric of Amish life was shaped by their dependence on the soil. In the words of one young farmer, "When you get away from working the soil, you get away from nature, and then you are getting away from the Lord's handiwork." What will happen as the Amish leave the farm? Will their whole way of life collapse?

Construction crews build residential and commercial facilities for both Amish and non-Amish alike.

The farm provided a seedbed for nurturing strong families in the values of hard work, frugality, responsibility, simplicity, and family cooperation. Farming was so important that for some years, persons risked excommunication from the church if they entered commercial or public work unrelated to agriculture. However, a small number of Amish have always been involved in non-farm work—traditional crafts and farm-related work such as blacksmithing and carpentry.

Why Don't All Amish Farm?

Non-farm work evolved in three stages. First, as cars became popular in American society, the Amish developed their own shops to manufacture and repair buggies and harnesses. Second, as tractors gained a monopoly in farming, the Amish developed machine shops to adapt tractor equipment for horses and to manufacture some of their own machinery. The third and largest jump in non-farming jobs came in the '70s and '80s as the Amish set up small manufacturing shops and cottage industries.

In recent years, the Amish have found themselves caught in a dilemma between shrinking farmland and soaring population growth. Their population is doubling every 20 years. Improved medicines, a high birth rate, rejection of birth control, and effective socialization have fueled Amish growth. As their population rises, farmland vanishes. Industrialization, suburbanization, and tourism have boosted Lancaster County's economy and nibbled away at the farmland. The Amish have coped with this demographic squeeze in several ways. Between 1940 and 1975 they planted nearly a dozen new settlements in other Pennsylvania counties. Today some 4,000 persons in the younger settlements trace their lineage back to the parent settlement. The Amish also subdivided farms into two or three smaller ones with intensive and specialized agriculture.

The Threat of Factory Work

Migration and subdivision, however, were not enough. Without high school and professional training, members

Hundreds of small cottage industries yield homemade products to sell at roadside stands.

found factory work a tempting alternative. Church leaders opposed factory work for a variety of reasons. "The lunch pail," said one bishop, "is the greatest threat to our whole way of life." Why did the bishops fear factory work? They worried it would break up families by separating spouses and by separating fathers from their children. The father's influence over the family would wane. His importance as a role model for children would shrink. Furthermore, the factory was a foreign cultural environment. Continuous interaction with outsiders could contaminate the values of even the most conscientious members.

Factory work threatened to undermine the Amish community in other ways as well. Health insurance and pension plans provided by employers would free individuals from their dependence on the community. In the long run, this would dismantle the historic practice of mutual aid within the Amish community. Corporate personnel policies made it difficult for Amish persons to participate in barn-raisings, work frolics, and weddings as they freely did when they were farming. For all these reasons the bishops frowned on factory work. But with scarce land and few technical or professional skills, where would Amish youth find work?

Small Industries Sustain Values

In the late '70s and '80s a happy solution emerged. Small industries and manufacturing shops offered a way out of the quandary. They permitted the Amish to enter non-farm work without carrying a lunch pail off to a "foreign" factory. The new development was a compromise of sorts. After nearly three centuries of farming, the Amish were able to leave their plows behind without embracing factory work. They agreed to go halfway and shift occupational gears, if they could do it on their own terms. They would control the conditions and terms of their non-farm work. By setting up over 1,000 industries, they are able to regulate the cultural environment of their work. The microenterprises are typically profitable; many boast annual sales above $500,000.

Today, more than half of married Amishmen work in non-farm jobs. In some church districts the number climbs over 70 percent. Many single men and women also earn their living away from the farm. About 20% of the businesses are owned and operated by women. (Married women rarely hold full-time jobs away from home.) Four types of Amish industries predominate. First, cottage industries located on a farm or beside a new home employ a half dozen or fewer family members and/or neighbors in crafts, repair work, or light manufacturing. Second, larger shops manufacture farm machinery, lawn furniture, storage sheds, and a variety of other products. They may hire as many as 10 employees. Third, mobile carpentry and construction crews crisscross Lancaster County and travel to adjoining counties to construct homes, install kitchens, and build silos. Finally, many Amish also operate retail stores that sell hardware, clothing, furniture, appliances, and crafts. These stores serve the Amish community as well as their non-Amish neighbors and tourists. Products ranging from clumsy manure spreaders to dainty cornhusk dolls are produced and sold by the community.

Amish machine shops manufacture implements for both Amish and non-Amish farmers.

The rise of Amish industries has enriched community life. Work remains near the home. Thus family members often work together, preserving traditional patterns of child-rearing and interaction. The network of shops creates a cloistered environment where fellow members interact and perpetuate an Amish world. Amish ownership of businesses offers employees greater freedom to participate in community affairs—mutual aid, barn-raisings, weddings, and other social events. Amish control eliminates adverse personnel policies which might undercut the traditional patterns of Amish life. The spread of Amish shops and stores creates an ethnic network where church members can trade commodities with each other. This fortifies the economic fabric of the community. This economic web keeps financial resources within community channels since many necessities can be bought from an Amish store. Amish shops have also bolstered the economic vitality of their community through sales to outsiders.

The diversity of Amish shops offers a new array of jobs to Amish youth. One old sage said, "About the only thing we don't have is an undertaker." Yet compared to modern life, the range of occupational choices is narrow. An Amish young person's lack of high school, professional training, and driver's license eliminates thousands of jobs. Moreover, jobs which violate traditional norms are taboo. Repairing television sets or selling jewelry, for instance, would not be permissible. Jobs that involve frequent interaction with outsiders—selling real estate, operating a video store, owning a restaurant—are not fitting.

An Occupational Buffer

What will be the impact of the shift to non-farm work? The occupational shift may lead to a three-tier social class of farmers, entrepreneurs, and day laborers. The long-term consequences are difficult to anticipate. In many ways the small industries and shops permit the Amish to perpetuate their traditional rural culture in a new setting where work remains local, communal, family centered, and lodged in an ethnic context. Avoiding factory and professional work, the Amish have created an occupational buffer between their culture and the outside world. On the other hand, the business owners represent a new commercial class of Amishmen who are bright, wealthy, and worldly in many ways. Will they continue to invest their hefty profits back into the life of the church community? Will they be satisfied, over the years, with the slow pace and traditional stance of Amish life? In the meantime, at least, the occupational shift has bolstered the vitality of Amish life.

15.
Education

Puzzle: Why do the Amish use the services of professionals—lawyers, doctors, and dentists—but oppose higher education?

The Amish have never prohibited the use of medicine, but like many rural folks they do not run to the doctor for every illness. Medical practices vary considerably by family. Some parents take their children to the doctor on a regular basis while others go only in the case of extreme emergency. The Amish use modern medicines, but they also rely on folk remedies. They have no religious objections to entering hospitals but are more likely than most modern Americans to "let nature have its way." In the '50s and '60s most Amish babies were born in hospitals, but in recent years many have been born at home with the assistance of a certified midwife or in a birthing clinic at a doctor's office. Since Amish children do not attend public schools they are less likely to be immunized for polio or measles. Some parents immunize their children on schedule while others do so only when threatened by a polio or measles epidemic. Orthodontic treatment, rarely done for aesthetic purposes, is used to correct serious malformations.

The Amish tap the services of many other professionals. Businessmen and some farmers routinely use lawyers to handle real estate transactions and to prepare business agreements. Professional accountants provide assistance on a reg-

Students are often called "scholars" in the Amish community.

ular basis to Amish businessmen. Veterinarians and other technicians typically offer state-of-the-art consultation to Amish farmers.

As farms and businesses expanded, the Amish were forced to rely on these professionals or risk severe economic loss. The Amish thought it was better to utilize the professional services of others than to send their children off to college and risk losing them. But why shun education? Why not allow some of their children to pursue higher education so they could provide professional services to their own people?

The Problem with Higher Education

The Amish are not opposed to education per se, but they disdain public education and higher education that would pull children away from their families and their traditions. In the words of one Amishman, "We're not opposed to education. We're just against education higher than our heads. I mean education that we don't need." In the Amish view, a practical, down-to-earth elementary education is adequate to prepare Amish youth for success in Amish culture. Until 1950, Amish students attended one-room, public schools. Such an education was compatible with Amish values. Teachers were familiar with the rural culture, and in some schools Amish youth were the majority.

As public schools consolidated and state attendance laws tightened, the Amish began to protest. Even with work permits, youth were required to attend until 15 years of age, which usually meant going to ninth grade. Amish protest galvanized. Dozens of parents were arrested and imprisoned each fall (1950-1955) for refusing to send their children to consolidated elementary schools and to public high schools. To the Amish, an eighth grade education, anchored in the classic three R's, was an adequate preparation for Amish life. They wanted their children in a local school where they would be taught by local teachers sympathetic to Amish values. They opposed busing their children away to a strange environment. Science education, evolution, sex education, and critical analysis threatened the traditional Amish world view. Physical education was deemed unnecessary and superfluous. The use of television in elementary schools was particularly irksome to the Amish.

Consolidated elementary schools and public high schools would expose Amish children to threatening values—individualism, competition, rational thinking, secularism—which in the long run would undermine Amish life. Moreover, Amish youth would develop significant friendships with outsiders at a key time in their lives. A high school education that stressed critical thinking and rational analysis would surely encourage Amish youth to question traditional Amish values and lead them off the farm. Many would likely end up in college or in professional occupations and be lost to the church forever.

An Amish School System Develops

The clash between Amish parents and school authorities in the early '50s led to two developments: the rise of Amish parochial schools and the beginning of a vocational program. Rather than send their children to consolidated elementary

Amish schools are built, cleaned, and maintained by local Amish community members.

Schools immerse pupils in a world of Amish values.

schools, church leaders decided to operate their own one-room schools. In some cases they bought one-room schools as the public townships sold them in public auctions. In other cases they built their own. Students attended one-room Amish schools through the eighth grade. State law, however, required compulsory attendance until age 15. This meant Amish youth had to attend ninth grade in a public high school—a requirement their parents vigorously opposed.

After several years of discussion, Amish leaders and public officials hammered out a compromise that complied with the compulsory school law without forcing Amish youth to attend public high school. Called the Amish Vocational Program, the compromise permits Amish 14-year-olds to attend a weekly vocational school in an Amish home after completing eighth grade in their parochial school. For three hours a week, an Amish teacher instructs a dozen or so youth in practical vocational skills, business math, reading, and writing. Students keep a diary of their work activities throughout the week which the teacher also reviews.

In 1972, the U.S. Supreme Court conferred its legal blessing on Amish schools. This legal victory for the Amish ended disputes in several states and stabilized the Amish school system. Today, Amish children attend some 150 one-room Amish elementary schools in the Lancaster settlement. With an average of 30 pupils, the schools are often within walking distance of the child's home. A local school board of parents supervises school policies and hires the teachers, typically single Amish women. Graduates themselves of the Amish schools, the teachers are chosen for their academic ability and commitment to religious values and Amish views. The school curriculum emphasizes basic skills—reading, writing, spelling, geography, and practical math. Both German and English are taught. Although schools have devotional exercises, religion is considered too sacred to be taught in a formal way. The Amish believe religious faith should be taught by parents in the home and by the church.

Amish schools have been remarkably successful in preparing youth for productive lives within Amish society. The Amish objection to high school and college remains firm. Few youth show interest in attending high school. Members who attend college risk excommunication. By limiting exposure to unorthodox ideas and restricting social interaction with outside peers, the schools preserve traditional ways and steer youth toward adult involvement in the Amish community.

By using the services of outside professionals, the Amish have been able to strengthen their community and adapt to modern life without risking the loss of their children. It was a compromise that allowed the Amish to keep pace with modern ways without jeopardizing traditional values or sacrificing their children on the altar of progress. If Amish children attend public high school and college, they might dramatically change the church or leave it entirely. Rational thinking, taught by public schools, breeds individualism which threatens core Amish values—submission, self-surrender, humility, and obedience. To preserve their traditional culture and prevent the loss of their children, the Amish were forced to snub public education. Willing, however, to compromise with modern life, they agreed to tap the services of outside professionals to strengthen and enhance their community.

16.
Wild Oats

Puzzle: Why do Amish youth rebel in their teenage years?

Trained to be meek and mild in Amish schools, youth sometimes sow wild oats in their teenage years. Despite extolling the virtues of obedience, parents and leaders overlook some of the rebellious antics. Many of the rowdy youth eventually become compliant, adult church members. Why does this quiet culture, this cradle of meekness and humility, tolerate an outburst of rebellion in teenage years?

In their late teens, youth often join a "crowd" of Amish youth numbering as many as a hundred or more. Several crowds, with various reputations, crisscross the settlement. Some crowds conform to traditional Amish ways. These youth attend Sunday evening singings and engage in traditional recreation—softball, volleyball, sledding, hiking, and skating. Other crowds openly flout the teachings of the church. The more rowdy groups have barn parties called hoedowns. Wilder parties often involve alcohol. Amish youth are occasionally arrested for possession of alcohol and sometimes charged with drunken driving of both buggies and cars.

Some boys own cars in open violation of Amish teachings. One Amishman estimated that 30 percent of the boys own cars, 40 percent have a driver's license and perhaps as high as 70 percent drive at one time or another. Some crowds rent public roller skating rinks for parties. Smaller clusters attend movies together or travel to professional baseball games.

Like other youth, Amish teens sometimes rebel. Wearing wristwatches and neglecting hats, these fellows seem to have fun in mind.

Others go to the beach or deep sea fishing. Still others may take a weekend fling to New York City.

Amish youth often discard their traditional dress on a weekend away. Boys will cut their hair in contemporary fashion, wear store-bought clothing, and toss off their Amish hats. Freed of their ethnic badges, they blend smoothly into public crowds without notice. In some cases their deviance is carefully hidden. They park their cars out of sight in rented space at a nearby garage. In other instances, youth openly mock church rules.

Is It Hypocrisy?

Non-Amish neighbors call this youthful deviance a glaring hypocrisy in Amish life and criticize the Amish for not "clamping down" on their offspring. Church leaders themselves are embarrassed by the foolishness. Some parents try to curb the antics of their teenagers while others merely look the other way. Scholars sometimes call the sowing of wild oats a "social problem." In any event, it is a perplexing puzzle that appears to contradict the basic tenets of Amish life. Why does this blemish on Amish culture persist?

The Amish church takes adult baptism quite seriously. Youth are typically baptized between 16 and 21 years of age, girls often a few years before boys. Baptism is a requirement for marriage. Candidates for baptism vow on their knees to follow the teachings and practices of the church. This is a serious commitment. Those who openly transgress their baptismal vow are asked to repent and make a public confession. Stubborn deviants who show no remorse risk excommunication and eventually shunning. Prior to baptism, the church has little social control over members of the community. Unbaptized teenagers sowing their wild oats are not under the thumb of the church. They cannot be asked to make confessions, nor can they be excommunicated or shunned. Thus the years between childhood and adult membership in Amish society are a transitional moment when youth are betwixt and between—neither in nor out of the church.

A Long-Term Benefit

Sowing wild oats plays a social role in the larger scheme of things, which is likely the reason it persists. The opportunity to sow wild oats gives Amish youth a chance to accept or reject the culture of their birthright. It offers a moment to explore the outside world, to experiment and to rebel before submitting to the regulations of the church. Prior to baptism they may leave the church without the fear of excommunication or shunning. This is their moment of choice, their chance to decide whether or not they want to be Amish. Surprisingly, more than 80 percent, or four out of five, eventually choose to stay Amish.

The wild oats syndrome gives Amish youth an apparent choice, but in reality it is more of a perceived choice than a real one. Several factors account for that. First, Amish child-rearing funnels youth in the direction of church membership. Young people have spent their entire lives within the confines of the Amish institutions. They have been culturally programmed to become Amish . To leave their cultural habitat at this age would be the equivalent of pulling up roots and moving to a foreign country. Second, all their close friends and family are within the Amish community. To leave would mean severing their most intimate ties. Third, romance often provides an important emotional tug. To marry they must be baptized members. Several youth reported that the prospect of marriage played an important role in their decision to join the church. Fourth, economic incentives also beckon. A son or son-in-law may have the offer of a farm or business partnership with convenient financing. Fifth, Amish youth without academic degrees and skilled training would find it difficult to compete for professional jobs in the larger society. And finally, of course, genuine spiritual reasons also lead youth to baptism. All of these factors, in concert, prod Amish youth toward church membership.

Despite the fact that their choice may not be completely free and open, the perception of choice is crucial. For if Amish youth believe that they have a choice, they will more likely be willing to comply with church regulations as adults. If they thought they had no choice in the matter in the first place, they might be less willing to conform to the rules of the church in adult life. Thus, the sowing of wild oats reaps a bountiful harvest of compliant adults for the church because they believe that, after all, they did have a choice. They decided to make the baptismal vow on their knees and promised to support the church. The bounteous yield of obedient adults is likely the reason why the puzzle of wild oats persists in Amish life.

17.
Freeloading

Puzzle: Are the Amish freeloading on American life?

The Amish enjoy many benefits of modern science and technology. Their robust growth rate flows, in part, from the achievements of modern medicine. Yet they have contributed neither people nor ideas to science. They benefit from public programs like everyone else, but do they pay their fair share? Are they freeloaders, social parasites of sorts, that feed off the larger social system without contributing an equal share?

In many ways the Amish are freeloaders in the American system. They have achieved in farming by building upon the insights of veterinary science and agricultural research. Productive Amish shops and industries tap the inventory of scientific knowledge in the larger society. Without penicillin and other advances in medicine, Amish mortality rates would rise, choking off their booming growth. In all these ways and many more, the Amish have benefited from modern science and technology without contributing to them. By avoiding science in their schools and forbidding their children to pursue scientific careers, they snub science, the hallmark of modernity.

In a similar fashion they remain aloof from the political system that guarantees the very religious liberties that allow them to be different in the first place. Although some vote, the Amish avoid public office and refrain from other political activities. They refuse to serve in the military that protects

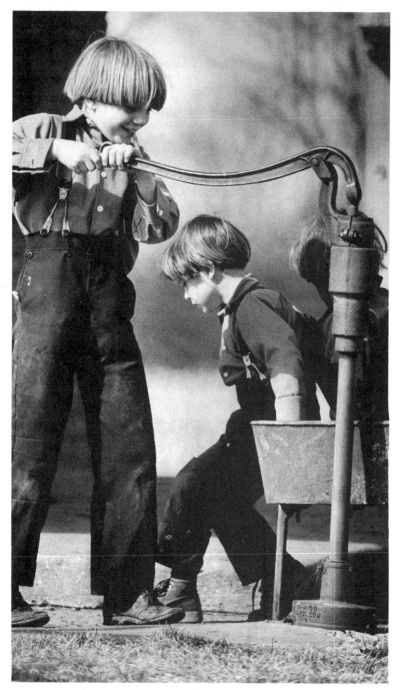

The Amish have historically stressed self-sufficiency.

the religious freedom they applaud and cherish. They pull their children out of school after eighth grade, thwart their potential to exclude them from professional occupations which could contribute to the public good. The Amish do not participate in community service organizations—Rotary, Lions, Kiwanis, and Jaycees—all of which enhance the public welfare. The very existence of Amish society rests on a tolerant political system—one to which they give meager support.

Although their existence hinges on political tolerance from other Americans, they show little tolerance toward deviants within their own ranks. Indeed, the larger society is used as a human rubbish pile of sorts for the castoffs from Amish life. Amish who are self-employed or working for Amish employers are exempt from Social Security taxes which could assist the destitute and elderly in the larger world. Amish horses chop up public roadways, but their owners pay no gasoline tax to support road repair. In all these ways, the Amish have been freeloading, enjoying the benefits of modern life without paying for them. Is there, however, another side to this story?

Contributors or Leeches?

The contention that the Amish are social parasites is a warped view of this puzzle. In fact, the Amish might argue that they pay more than their fair share. Like other Americans, they pay taxes—real estate, income, sales—as well as a variety of local and state taxes. Indeed, the Amish pay school taxes twice. Their real estate taxes support public schools which they do not use. They also underwrite the costs of their own schools.

The Amish, of course, do not pay gasoline taxes. Self employed members and those who work for Amish employers are exempt from Social Security. The exempt do not receive any Social Security or medical benefits (medicare and medicaid) which, all in all, is a fair exchange. Non-Amish employers must pay Social Security taxes for Amish employees who receive nothing in return from the Social Security

The community relies on mutual aid rather than federal subsidies in the face of disaster.

system. In any event, the Amish do not feed off the Social Security system. Some in fact, contribute to it with no return. The Amish object to Social Security because they believe church members should care for one another's needs. Reliance on government retirement programs, they fear, would undermine the Amish system of mutual aid and violate the principle of separation from the world.

Through a variety of taxes the Amish contribute millions of dollars into public coffers, but they use few public services. Their tax dollars, like other citizens', support scientific research and military programs. Although they do not teach science in their schools, the Amish have willingly served as human subjects in a variety of research programs designed to trace the genetic transmission of disease over several generations. Large families, good genealogical records, and little mobility make the Amish an ideal population for such studies.

Besides objecting to Social Security, the Amish have also declined to accept funds from federally subsidized agricultural programs. With a strong tradition of mutual help within their community, they believe in self-sufficiency and independence from government programs. They are, in their words, "opposed to government hand-out programs." Besides turning down farm subsidies, the Amish use fewer public services than most Americans. Their members do not receive welfare checks, and they rarely sit in jail. Amish youth do not borrow federal funds for college. Adults use few public services because of their rural setting and strong community tradition of mutual aid. Members rarely use Medicare for expensive medical treatment. Although they are taxed along with everyone else, the Amish, on the average, use fewer public services. Perhaps, then, the larger world is freeloading, taking more from the Amish than it returns to them?

What about Conscientious Objection?

The Amish are conscientious objectors who will not serve in the military because of their religious beliefs. In World War II and after, many Amish youth received farm deferments while others participated in some form of alternate public service. Certainly this is freeloading. How could freedom be protected if everyone did the same? Rather than speculate about hypothetical military outcomes, the Amish believe they must be obedient to the teachings of the Bible, the way of Jesus and their consciences, regardless of the consequences. In their own way they have contributed to a peace-

An Amishman taps the benefits of modern technology.

Amish parents pay taxes for public schools as well as for their own.

ful world order by creating a society where violence is prohibited, where patience, not force, is the norm, and where confession, not retaliation, is esteemed. Such a community does not directly contribute to the national defense. It is, instead, a powerful reminder that there are other ways of structuring human behavior. In the long run such examples may contribute as much, if not more, to national security and global understanding as threats to use nuclear weapons.

The Irony of Tourism

The rise of tourism brought an ironic twist in Amish relations with the larger world—a twist that surely relieves them of the freeloader stigma. The more they resist modern culture, the more interesting they become to the rest of us. The number of tourists visiting Amish communities has surged in recent years. In Lancaster County alone, some five million tourists visit annually, spending over 400 million dollars—the equivalent of $29,000 for each Amish person. Tourism in Lancaster County does not rest totally on the Amish, but they are a major focus. If the Amish evacuated the area, tourist revenue would surely plummet. Tourist income bolsters local and state taxes. In fact, gasoline taxes paid by tourists certainly exceed the amount the Amish would ever pay if they were driving cars.

The tourist industry creates hundreds of jobs and in many ways contributes to the economic well-being of the community. In any event, the Amish, once persecuted by the outside world, have now become an object of curiosity and often respect. Far from being social parasites, the Amish and their unique culture fuel a thriving tourist industry, all of which creates an ironic zigzag in the freeloading puzzle. For today, the larger community, especially in Lancaster County, leans on the Amish not only for its image and reputation, but also as a major source of revenue.

18.
Progress

Puzzle: **Are the Amish behind or ahead of the modern world?**

In many ways the Amish lag behind the rest of the world. They scorn the latest fads and mock the spirit of progress. Customary ways seem to make more sense to them than modern ones. They extol traditional thinking over abstract analysis. They drag their cultural feet, hoping to tame the powerful forces of progress. But are they really behind the rest of us, or might they indeed be ahead? That is the puzzle of progress. In any event, the Amish prod us to ask whether modern life is a step forward or backward? Is progress really progress?

The modern age has brought us stunning scientific achievements ranging from genetic engineering to space travel. Modern thinking has fractured the underpinnings of oppressive political systems pivoting on racism, sexism, and caste. Modern life has liberated humans from a variety of oppressions and ushered in an enormous spectrum of options for personal achievement and success. The possibilities for human advancement and personal fulfillment are endless. But the modern era has also levied a social-psychological toll on the human community. The price of progress, in other words, has been high—escalating divorce rates, climbing numbers of suicides, greater alienation, sky-rocketing drug abuse, rising domestic violence, and pervasive stress—just a few of the indicators of modern ills. The

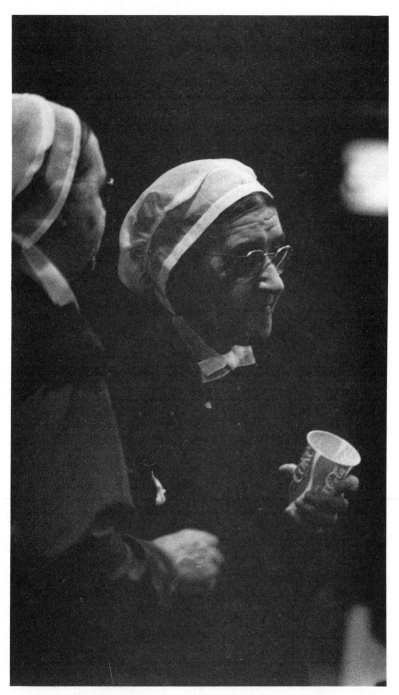

Modern and traditional symbols merge in Amish life.

panorama of choices facing individuals in the modern world brings a certain liberation. The incessant decision-making also increases the burden of anxiety, and with it, the number of trips to the therapist's office. Thus the story of progress is a mixed tale.

The price of contentment in Amish life has also been high, for it means surrendering individualism and bridling personal aspirations. Modern culture and Amish thinking clash on their views of personal fulfillment. The key to human contentment and fulfillment for modern folks lies in personal freedom. Choice and independence bring exhilaration and satisfaction. In contrast, the Amish believe that personal fulfillment is found as people lose themselves in their faith community. True personhood is discovered as one yields to the larger body, a practical demonstration of one's Christian commitment. The Amish have not joined the modern world, for they limit the choices of individual members. The range of choice in Amish life—from clothing to transportation, from lifestyles to occupations—is remarkably narrow. Traditional sex roles, a parochial world view, frugality, and

The restriction on cars creates inconvenience but uses less gas and lowers exhaust pollution.

118

Home is the place where most Amish people work—farming, gardening, or producing food, furniture, and handcrafts for sale.

discipline permeate the culture. Obedience takes priority over individualism. Conformity is the norm, not freedom. Work is esteemed over leisure and convenience. In all of these ways, the Amish have not clamored after the spirit of progress.

Who Is More Free?

Few outsiders have been willing to join the Amish and forgo personal freedoms for the emotional securities of a stable social order. The Amish have curtailed individualism in order to preserve community, contentment, and continuity. But the limits to freedom have brought other freedoms in disguise. The Amish are not free to buy the latest model car of their choice, but they are free from monotonous hours of commuting on crowded freeways. They are not free to buy a fashionable dress, but they are free from the anxiety of dressing for success. They are not free to pursue professional occupations, but they are free to determine their own hours and pace of work. The Amish are not free to go to college, but they are free from worry about retirement in old age. They are not free to violate community standards, but they are free from endless trips to the therapist's office.

The price of contentment in Amish life—the surrender of personal aspirations to faith community goals—is high. But in return, members receive a durable identity, a sense of belonging to a distinctive people, a meaningful world view, a keen sense of social roots, and unwavering emotional security. These basic fibers of the human fabric have often frayed in the face of progress. What the Amish lose in individualism they gain in community, identity, and belonging. What they lose in freedom they gain in a stable and dependable social order.

Who Is More Fulfilled?

Without the aid of consultants or the benefits of higher education, they have created a different world, a world without welfare recipients, homeless vagabonds, and illegitimate children. A world where stress workshops are unknown and where drug and alcohol abuse are almost nil. A world where divorce is unknown, truancy is unheard of, and violent crime is rare. The Amish world of frugality and simplicity defies modern trends of energy consumption and waste. In time of

A slower pace offers time for conversation.

fire, disaster, or special need, a spontaneous Amish social security system springs into action. Work, in Amish life, continues to bear the mark of craftsmanship, integrity, and personal identity. The small-scale size of Amish life assures each individual a warm emotional home—a niche in a stable social order. The Amish have shaped a community that defies the trends of modern societies, but one which nevertheless fulfills basic human needs in profound ways. By negotiating with modern life, the Amish have bypassed the pitfalls of progress while tapping enough of its resources to maintain a viable community. In all these ways the Amish press us to explore the meaning of progress and ponder what it means to be "ahead" or "behind."

Make no mistake, these are not a perfect people. Marriages do sour, and greed and pride lift their heads here as in any human community. The powerful sometimes maneuver the flow of events to achieve selfish goals. Rebellious youth embarrass family and leaders alike. Family feuds sometimes mar the tranquility of an otherwise peaceful community. Incest and domestic abuse occasionally occur. These people are people. But despite their shortcomings, they have created a social order in which human contentment flourishes.

What is progress? If progress means the use of the latest electronic technology, the vigorous pursuit of personal goals, the protection and celebration of individual rights, ultra conveniences, a preoccupation with leisure, an unwavering belief in scientific research to solve human problems, the erosion of religious faith, the scorn of tradition, and a delight in consumerism, then surely the Amish are lagging behind.

However, if progress means emotional security, freedom from the anxiety of choice, a lack of worry in the face of old age and disaster, stable family ties, social equality, control of the conditions and terms of one's work, and if it means delighting in craftsmanship, limiting the negative effects of technology, preserving peoplehood and community, cultivating durable social ties, and bestowing religious meaning on all of life, then perhaps the Amish are indeed ahead.

It is easy to romanticize Amish life as an idyllic alternative to modern ways. But even Amish life would be dismal without the benefits of higher education, advanced technology, and scientific research. Neither the Amish, nor the rest of us, would want to live in a world without the blessings of science. And yet modern life with all its achievements has brought its own share of social blight.

A comparison of Amish and modern ways raises the bigger puzzle of progress. Is it possible to fashion a world where human intellect and curiosity are celebrated—where education and science flourish—but where cancerous individualism, greed, and inequality are banned? Such a world would mean tighter restraints on individual rights for moderns, and greater flexibility in intellectual freedom for the Amish. Real progress would bring the best of both worlds together, the technique and expertise of modernity, as well as the continuity and contentment of a faith community's traditional ways.

Readings and Sources

Fisher, Gideon. *Farm Life and Its Changes.* Gordonville, Pennsylvania: Peaquea Publishers, 1978.

Fisher, Sara E. and Rachel K. Stahl. *The Amish School.* Intercourse, Pennsylvania: Good Books, 1986.

Good, Merle. *Who Are the Amish?* Intercourse, Pennsylvania: Good Books, 1985.

Good, Merle and Phyllis. *20 Most Asked Questions about the Amish and Mennonites.* Intercourse, Pennsylvania: Good Books, 1997.

Hostetler, John A. *Amish Society.* Baltimore: Johns Hopkins University Press, 1980.

Kraybill, Donald B. *The Riddle of Amish Culture.* Baltimore: Johns Hopkins University Press, 1989.

____, ed. *The Amish and the State.* Baltimore: Johns Hopkins University Press, 1993.

Kraybill, Donald B. *Old Order Amish: Their Enduring Way of Life.* Baltimore: Johns Hopkins University Press, 1993.

Kraybill, Donald B. and Steven M. Nolt. *Amish Enterprise: From Plows to Profits.* Baltimore: Johns Hopkins University Press, 1995.

Kraybill, Donald B. and Marc Olshan. *The Amish Struggle with Modernity.* Hanover, New Hampshire: University Press of New England, 1994.

Nolt, Steven M. *A History of the Amish.* Intercourse, Pennsylvania: Good Books, 1992.

Scott, Stephen E. *Why Do They Dress That Way?* Intercourse, Pennsylvania: Good Books, 1986.

Scott, Stephen E. and Kenneth Pellman. *Living Without Electricity.* Intercourse, Pennsylvania: Good Books, 1990.

Yoder, Paton. *Tradition and Transition: Amish Mennonites and Old Order Amish, 1800-1900.* Scottdale, Pennsylvania: Herald Press, 1990.

About the Author

Donald B. Kraybill is professor of Sociology and Anabaptist-Pietist Studies at Messiah College (Grantham, PA), where he also serves as provost. He is the author of *The Riddle of Amish Culture, Old Order Amish, Amish Enterprise: From Plows to Profits,* and the editor of *The Amish and the State,* all published by Johns Hopkins University Press. He has also co-authored *The Amish Struggle with Modernity,* published by the University Press of New England.